QUIZWHIZ 4

NATIONAL
GEOGRAPHIC
KiDS

QUIZ
WHIZ 4

1,000 SUPER FUN MIND-BENDING TOTALLY AWESOME TRIVIA QUESTIONS

NATIONAL GEOGRAPHIC
WASHINGTON, D.C.

Table of CONTENTS

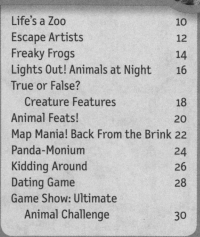

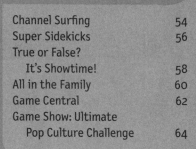

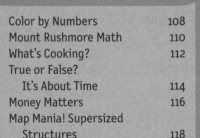
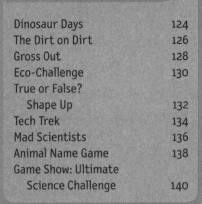
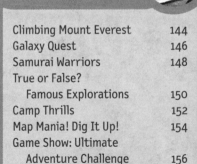

INTRODUCTION

Get your brain cells working! Pit your wits against our question masters, flex your mental muscles, and test your knowledge on more than 1,000 questions. Go on a page-turning journey of discovery to reveal what you know—and don't know—about animals, geography, nature, history, science, pop culture, math, and amazing adventures. Discover fascinating facts, learn about incredible people, and be amazed by awesome natural wonders.

Quiz Whiz 4 is packed with fascinating and funny questions. Do you know how many different languages are spoken in the world? Is Ping-Pong an Olympic sport? Is a cuttlefish a fish? What percentage of people in the world have mobile phones? What are pigeon droppings used for? You'll know the answers to these questions—and hundreds more—by the end of this book.

There are many different kinds of quiz games inside. Multiple-choice questions give you four possible answers to choose from. "True or False?" quizzes ask you to guess if each of the 30 theme-related random statements are fact or fiction.

"Map Mania!" quizzes ask you to locate animal habitats, where famous people lived, or where to see the biggest, tallest, or longest structures in the world on the map. More true-or-false questions throughout the book cover movies and TV, celebrities, dinosaurs, dangerous animals, record breakers, villains, food, inventions, and weird places. Each chapter ends with a "Game Show," where you'll find special photo questions and an extra-challenging "Ultimate Brain Buster."

The answers to all the questions are at the end of the book. Check your answers for one quiz or for all the quizzes in a chapter, then tally your score. Did you hit the jackpot or find your brain was on walkabout? If your brain starts to fizz, take a break and come back when your batteries are recharged. If you are on a roll, press on and go for a record-breaking run!

When you have become an expert, quiz your friends and parents and find out if they are quiz whizers! Tally your scores for each chapter and see who knows the most about each subject. It doesn't matter if you don't get all the answers correct. Remembering the answers and learning new things is your ultimate reward.

Animal QUEST

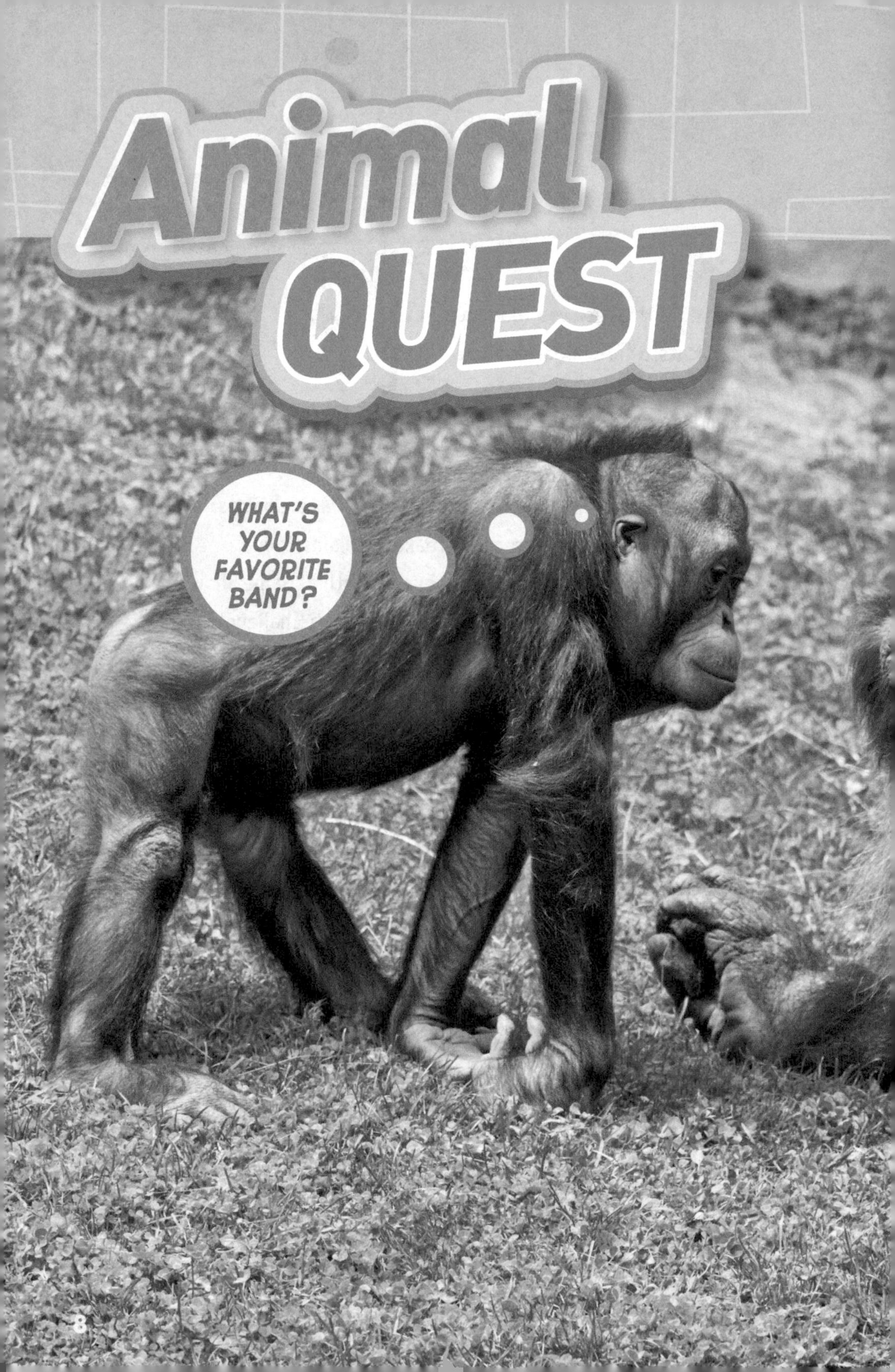

ORANGUTAN

9

Life's a zoo

CHEETAH

8✓ 3✗

1 Which of the following animals can reach faster speeds than a cheetah?
a. a horse
b. a great white shark
c. a gray squirrel
d. a red-tailed hawk ✓

2 Which type of elephant typically takes on a leadership role in a herd?
a. the one with the biggest tusks
b. a large male
c. an elder female
d. the one voted most likely to succeed

3 What is another name for an adult male gorilla?
a. silverback
b. big bubba
c. King Kong
d. ape-zilla

MALE GORILLA

4 True or false? More tigers live in captivity than in the wild.

5 What do elephants use their trunks to do?
a. breathe underwater
b. dig in the dirt
c. care for calves
d. all of the above

6 Seals, sea lions, and walruses are all "pinnipeds," which means ____.
a. dog fish
b. big tooth
c. wing-footed
d. pea brain

MALE LION

MALE LION

7 Which giant cat species has spots?

a. cougar
b. leopard
c. tiger
d. caracal

8 What is a flamingo's nest made out of?

a. leaves
b. mud
c. seashells
d. pink fluff

9 **True or false?** Males in a pride of lions do most of the hunting.

10 Which of these animals is usually afraid of swimming?

a. giant panda
b. giraffe
c. elephant
d. orangutan

RING-TAILED LEMUR

11 **True or false?** Six-foot-eight (2-m) basketball star LeBron James could walk under a giraffe without having to duck.

12 Which country is the native home for ring-tailed lemurs?

a. Madagascar
b. Peru
c. India
d. Spain

CHECK YOUR ANSWERS ON PAGES 158–159.

ESCAPE ARTISTS

1 To what color does an arctic hare's fur turn in **winter** to help it hide from predators?

a. spotted   c. white
b. black   d. blue

2 An **octopus** off the coast of Indonesia has been observed **mimicking** which underwater creature?

a. a poisonous sea snake
b. a giant clam
c. a scuba diver
d. a piece of seaweed

OCTOPUS

3 What does the longest insect in the world closely **resemble?**

a. boa constrictor
b. stick
c. ball of yarn
d. giraffe

4 True or false? **Chameleons** change color to communicate with one another.

5 What does the **spiny leaf** insect look like?

a. dead leaves   c. a spiky ball
b. a palm tree   d. a starfish

6 Why do starlings fly together in **large** flocks?

a. to keep warm
b. to battle airplanes
c. to carry messages for secret agents
d. to confuse predators

7 Which **feature** evolved in some butterflies in Brazil to help them avoid getting eaten?

a. wing patterns that match those of poisonous butterflies
b. an extra set of wings
c. the ability to growl like hunting leopards
d. long, poisonous fangs

8 How do gazelles often **escape** from cheetahs, the fastest land animal?

a. they kick up rocks at them
b. they zigzag side to side
c. they build walls around their grazing grounds
d. they hide in the woods

9 For camouflage, the skin of pygmy seahorses changes to match the colors and textures of which part of its **environment?**

a. coral
b. seaweed
c. sand
d. sharks

11 What should you do to **escape** from a **bear** trying to defend its **territory?**

a. scream at the top of your lungs
b. play dead
c. climb a tree
d. run away as fast as you can

10 True or false? Pitcher plants shoot sticky tendrils to grab flying insects out of the **air.**

FREAKY FROGS

1 True or false?
The red-eyed tree frog
sleeps with its eyes open.

2 True or false?
Frogs use their
eyeballs to help
swallow prey.

RED-EYED
TREE FROG

3 Scientists found the world's tiniest
frog in New Guinea by _____ .

a. tempting the frogs with food
b. listening for their high-pitched calls
c. following birds to the frogs' hiding place
d. dressing up in frog suits

4 The Emberá people
in Colombia hunt
using frog venom on
which weapon?

a. knives
b. pointed sticks
c. blowgun darts
d. traps

6 How do male poison arrow
frogs help take care of their
young?

a. they spit poison at predators
b. they carry fertilized eggs and
tadpoles on their backs
c. they build little houses out of
sticks
d. they don't; only the females
care for the young

5 Where do female red-eyed tree
frogs lay their eggs?

a. at the bottom of a pond
b. on a leaf over the water
c. in a hole in the ground
d. in a sac that they carry around

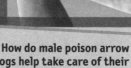

14

7 True or false?

A single golden poison dart frog has enough venom to kill ten adult humans.

8 What covers tree frogs' toes to help them climb and hang upside down?
a. sticky mucus
b. sharp spikes
c. superglue
d. Velcro

9 Amazon horned frogs hide under leaves on the forest floor. When a smaller creature comes close, they jump out and _____.
a. swallow it whole
b. pierce it with their horns
c. poison it with their bite
d. drag it under the leaves to save for later

10 The prehistoric devil frog was about the same size as which object?
a. paper clip
b. orange
c. pineapple
d. beach ball

11 What's the maximum amount of time Alaskan wood frogs can survive being frozen solid?
a. 15 minutes
b. 5 hours
c. 1 week
d. 2 months

12 Red-eyed tree frogs don't have webbed toes, so they don't usually go _____.
a. up trees
b. under rocks
c. in the water
d. onto leaves

13 Which body part of poison dart frogs is extremely toxic?
a. the skin
b. the tip of the tongue
c. the fangs
d. only the bright blue spots

14 How do most frogs get a drink?
a. their tongue rolls into a straw
b. their skin absorbs water
c. they catch rain in their mouths
d. they don't need water to survive

15 True or false?

All frogs use their tongues to catch insects.

CHECK YOUR ANSWERS ON PAGES 158–159.

LIGHTS OUT! Animals at Night

1 Which animal is *not* mostly nocturnal, or active at night?
- a. elephant
- b. bat
- c. firefly
- d. tiger

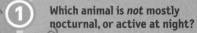

BAT

2 How do bats find their way around at night?
- a. they have X-ray vision
- b. they fly into things and bounce off
- c. they make clicking sounds and listen for echoes
- d. they remember where everything is

3 The kinkajou, a nocturnal type of raccoon also called a honey bear, uses its long, skinny tongue to _____ .
- a. spit water at people
- b. get honey from beehives
- c. hang upside down from branches
- d. catch birds out of the air

4 **True or false?** Cats' eyes glow in the dark.

5 What is this nighttime hunter, pictured left, called?
- a. snowy owl
- b. great horned owl
- c. barn owl
- d. cat-faced owl

6 The western diamondback rattlesnake hunts at night when the desert is cool. How does it locate its prey?
- a. it senses the prey's body heat
- b. its excellent hearing picks up noisy prey
- c. it flies by whipping its tail around to stalk prey
- d. it hypnotizes prey by rattling its tail

7 What does the night shark typically eat?

   a. squid and fish   **c.** fireflies

   b. seagulls   **d.** people

false

8 **True or false?** Moths flying around electric lights are trying to stay warm.

9 What color are most night-blooming flowers?

   a. black or dark blue

   b. purple

   c. white or pale green

   d. no flowers bloom at night

MOUNTAIN LION

10 The mountain lion hunts at night using its sensitive eyes and ears, but it _____.

   a. can't hear or see squirrels

   b. closes its eyes when it attacks

   c. hibernates during the winter

   d. has a weak sense of smell

11 Sensitive hairs on which body part of a scorpion help it sense prey moving at night?

   a. stinger

   b. face

   c. legs

   d. stomach

SCORPION

12 The Kauai cave wolf spider of Hawaii lives in almost total darkness. What is its most notable feature?

   a. it doesn't have eyes

   b. it has only three legs

   c. it has a giant stinger

   d. it has the longest fur of any spider

13 **True or false?** There are no nocturnal monkeys.

false

TRUE or FALSE?
Creature Features

1. BUTTERFLIES CAN SEE MORE COLORS THAN PEOPLE CAN.

2. PELICANS USE THE POUCH IN THEIR BEAKS TO STORE FISH FOR SNACKING ON LATER. T

3. THE TAPIR HAS FOUR TOES ON ITS FRONT FEET AND THREE TOES ON ITS BACK FEET.

4. HYENAS MARK THEIR TERRITORY BY RELEASING A SOUR-SMELLING PASTE.

5. THE MANTIS SHRIMP CAN SMASH THROUGH GLASS WITH ITS CLAWS.

6. FEMALE GREEN SEA TURTLES BURY THEIR EGGS IN THE SAND. T

7. GREAT WHITE SHARKS CAN SENSE BLOOD IN THE WATER FROM UP TO 10 MILES (16 KM) AWAY.

8. ALL MAMMALS HAVE FOUR LEGS. F

9. THE DROMEDARY CAMEL HAS TWO HUMPS.

10. A CROW NAMED BETTY CREATED AND USED A TOOL TO RETRIEVE FOOD.

11. PENGUINS CAN'T FLY. T

12. IF A VAMPIRE BAT BITES YOU, YOU'LL DIE INSTANTLY.

13. SPIDER MONKEYS HAVE USELESS TAILS.

14. AN ANACONDA CAN SWALLOW PREY TWICE THE SIZE OF ITS HEAD.

15. JAGUARS CAN'T SWIM. T

16 THE SNOW LEOPARD WRAPS ITS LONG TAIL AROUND ITSELF TO KEEP WARM AT NIGHT.

17 SEA OTTERS SOMETIMES HOLD HANDS TO KEEP FROM DRIFTING APART WHEN THEY SLEEP.

18 BIRDS ARE THE ONLY ANIMALS ALIVE TODAY WITH FEATHERS. F

19 THERE'S NO SUCH THING AS A FLYING FROG.

20 FIREFLIES ABSORB LIGHT FROM THE SUN DURING THE DAY TO HELP THEM GLOW AT NIGHT.

21 WEBBED FEET ALLOW ANIMALS TO SWIM FASTER.

22 HERONS USE THEIR LONG BEAKS TO GRAZE ON UNDERWATER PLANTS.

23 OSTRICHES HAVE THE BIGGEST EYES OF ANY LAND ANIMAL.

24 THE CALL OF THE KOOKABURRA, AN AUSTRALIAN BIRD, SOUNDS LIKE HUMAN LAUGHTER.

25 AN ELECTRIC EEL CAN GENERATE A BIGGER SHOCK THAN A WALL OUTLET.

26 ALL SNAKES ARE POISONOUS. F

27 NAKED MOLE RATS LIVE IN COLONIES SIMILAR TO THOSE OF BEES OR ANTS.

28 SEA TURTLES ARE IMMUNE TO THE POWERFUL POISON OF A BOX JELLYFISH.

29 A POLAR BEAR'S LARGE PAWS HELP IT CATCH SWIMMING PENGUINS. F

30 SKUNK SPRAY IS DEADLY TO COYOTES.

CHECK YOUR ANSWERS ON PAGES 158–159.

Animal FEATS!

SPERM WHALES DIVING

1 Sperm whales have to dive deep to catch squid, their preferred prey. Up to how long can a sperm whale hold its breath?

a. 10 minutes   c. 90 minutes
b. 20 minutes   d. 2 hours

RHINOCEROS BEETLE

2 **True or false?** A rhinoceros beetle can lift more for its size than a rhinoceros.

3 The African elephant can grow tusks more than 10 feet (3 m) long. What is a tusk?

a. a horn   c. a second nose
b. a tooth   d. a skull bone

AFRICAN ELEPHANT

4 Sociable weaver birds live in large groups. Up to how many birds share a single nest?

a. 25   c. 100
b. 60   d. 5,000

5 Which of these animals is intelligent enough to recognize itself in a mirror?

a. elephant
b. dolphin
c. orangutan
d. all of the above

HOWLER MONKEY

6 A howler monkey's loudest scream is as loud as a _____ .

a. clarinet   c. rock concert
b. hand drill   d. jet engine

7 Which creature can communicate with sounds that are too low-pitched for humans to hear?

a. frog
b. parrot
c. rhinoceros
d. mouse

8 **True or false?** In its 30-year lifetime, an average arctic tern flies six times the distance between Earth and the moon.

9 Which ocean creature can live longer than 500 years?

a. clam
b. octopus
c. shark
d. seahorse

10 This animal construction—a mound 25 feet (7.6 m) tall—contains a chimney to help air flow through. Which creature built it?

a. hummingbirds
b. prairie dogs
c. salamanders
d. termites

11 A male platypus can sting other animals with poisonous barbs on its _____.

a. hind legs
b. tail
c. tongue
d. belly

12 **True or false?** Flying fish can soar high enough to land on the deck of a ship.

FLYING
FISH

MAP MANIA!
BACK FROM THE BRINK

These animal species are all bouncing back from endangered or threatened status. Match each photo to the animal's habitat on the map.

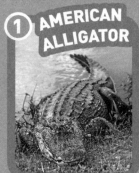

1 AMERICAN ALLIGATOR

2 ARABIAN ORYX

3 AMUR LEOPARD

4 CALIFORNIA CONDOR

5 CAPE MOUNTAIN ZEBRA

6 HELMETED HONEY EATER

D

NORTH AMERICA

PACIFIC OCEAN

I

L

C

F

E

ATLANTIC OCEAN

E

SOUTH AMERICA

A

7 LADYBIRD SPIDER

ARCTIC OCEAN

EUROPE

ASIA

D

J

K

B

AFRICA

PACIFIC OCEAN

E

E

INDIAN OCEAN

H

AUSTRALIA

G

ANTARCTICA

8 LEATHERBACK SEA TURTLE

11 NORTHERN SEA OTTER

10 NIGER GIRAFFE

9 RED WOLF

12 VICUÑA

CHECK YOUR ANSWERS ON PAGES 158–159.

PANDA-MONIUM

1 Which country do wild giant pandas call home?

a. Australia
b. Brazil
c. China
d. Zaire

2 Which of the following "bears" is not actually a member of the bear family?

a. panda bear
b. polar bear
c. koala bear
d. grizzly bear

3 How long does a panda bear hibernate during the winter months?

a. 2 weeks
b. 3 months
c. 6 months
d. they don't hibernate at all

4 True or false? Panda bears can stand and walk on their hind legs.

5 About how many giant pandas are left in the wild?

a. 140
b. 1,600
c. 9,500
d. 17,000

6 True or false? A panda bear can't eat anything other than bamboo.

7 Giant pandas in the wild spend most of their time ____.

a. alone
b. in pairs
c. in groups of 4 to 6
d. in tribes of 15 to 20

8 True or false?
When born, a baby panda is pink and white, with no black markings.

9 About how many heads of lettuce would you have to eat to match the amount of bamboo pandas in the wild consume each day?

a. 2
b. 9
c. 12
d. 28

10 *Daxiongmao*, the Chinese name for panda, translates to _____.

a. bamboo-eater
b. large bear cat
c. cuddly fuzzball
d. black-and-white beast

11 Which type of bear is the largest in the world?

a. giant panda
b. polar bear
c. teddy bear
d. Kodiak bear

12 True or false? Pandas have thumbs.

13 How many babies do mother panda bears typically have at one time?

a. 1 or 2
b. 2 to 5
c. 5 to 10
d. 10 or more

14 About how many hours each day does a panda spend eating?

a. 1   c. 12
b. 5   d. 18

15 What is the panda bear's natural habitat?

a. jungle   c. desert
b. mountain forest   d. grasslands

CHECK YOUR ANSWERS ON PAGES 158–159.

KIDDING AROUND

1 What is a **baby camel called?**

a. Humpty Dumpty
b. kid
c. puppy
d. calf

2 **True or false?**
A newborn baby elephant weighs more than most motorcycles.

3 What **color** are most newborn **baby mice?**

a. pink
b. white
c. blue-gray
d. brown

4 What is another name for a female **baby horse?**

a. colt
b. bonny
c. filly
d. doe

5 **How soon** after birth can **baby** giraffes stand up?

a. 5 minutes
b. 30 minutes
c. 4 hours
d. 2 days

6 **True or false?**
Nine-banded armadillos usually give birth to identical **quadruplets.**

7 What is the **main** reason that kittens play?

a. to learn how to hunt
b. to look adorable
c. to get on YouTube
d. to get warm

8 Which animal's baby is called a joey?

a. penguin
b. elephant
c. koala bear
d. hamster

9 If a newly hatched baby goose spends all of its time with a person, what is the goose likely **to do?**

a. learn to talk
b. eat lots of candy
c. think that person is its mother
d. attack all other geese

10 **True or false?** Baby caribou are born with antlers.

AFRICAN ELEPHANT

11 What do newborn blue whales **eat?**

a. their mother's milk
b. plankton
c. smaller whales
d. seaweed

12 How do mother kangaroos, wombats, and other marsupials carry their young?

a. in a backpack
b. in a pouch
c. in a nest
d. in an egg

13 Which of the following is **not a** stage that many baby insects go through?

a. egg
b. larva
c. pupa
d. tadpole

14 Which of the following is about the **same size** as a newborn **panda?**

a. jelly bean
b. stick of butter
c. loaf of bread
d. skateboard

CHECK YOUR ANSWERS ON PAGES 158–159.

Dating GAME

MOOSE

1 The larger a male moose's antlers are, the more likely it is that he _____.

a. is a healthy moose
b. will find a mate
c. will scare off other males
d. all of the above

2 Why did a male bowerbird gather all these blue objects together?

a. the bowerbird eats plastic
b. he decorated his nest to attract females
c. blue is the only color the bird can see
d. the objects scare away predators

BOWERBIRD NEST

3 **True or false?** Some female spiders eat the male after mating.

4 A manakin attracts a mate with a dance that looks like the moonwalk. What type of animal is it?

a. bird   c. goat
b. monkey   d. frog

5 Peahens, or female peacocks, tend to choose males with tails that feature the _____.

a. most different colors
b. largest eye spots
c. skinniest feathers
d. most fragrant smell

6 What do emperor penguins do just before they mate?

a. go for a swim
b. bow their heads to each other
c. build a snow fort
d. make a nest out of twigs

MALE PEACOCK

7 **True or false?** All whiptail lizards are female.

HUMPBACK WHALES

8 **What do male humpback whales do to attract females?**

a. sing together
b. put on cologne
c. catch lots of penguins
d. create necklaces of seashells

9 **In the Amazon River Basin, which animal might you see waving clumps of branches to attract a mate?**

a. grizzly bear
b. river dolphin
c. piranha
d. leopard

10 **What are these two male giraffes doing?**

a. fighting over a female giraffe
b. dancing with each other
c. waiting for it to rain
d. bragging about their girlfriends

11 **Many insects and other animals produce pheromones to help attract a mate from far away. What are pheromones?**

a. sharp horns
b. chemical signals
c. love songs
d. colorful feathers

12 **True or false?** A female chameleon turns brightly colored when she's ready to mate.

MALE GIRAFFES

CHECK YOUR ANSWERS ON PAGES 158–159.

GAME SHOW
ULTIMATE ANIMAL CHALLENGE

1 Which sound can mockingbirds mimic?
a. cricket chirps
b. a car alarm
c. a mewing cat
d. all of the above

2 TRUE OR FALSE?
Giant river otters can grow to 6 feet (1.8 m) in length.

3 At about what age does a wild Galápagos tortoise reach adulthood?
a. 1 to 2 years old
b. 2 to 10 years old
c. 10 to 20 years old
d. 20 to 40 years old

4 In Africa, researchers discovered a 600-pound (272-kg) creature. That's the biggest ever for which animal?
a. anteater   c. lizard
b. wild pig   d. bird

5 What does a male gentoo penguin give to his mate?
a. a pet turtle
b. a smooth pebble
c. a diamond ring
d. a stinging jellyfish

6 When it glows, what is the bobtail squid disguising itself as?
a. a shark   c. a starry sky
b. a firefly   d. Batman

7 TRUE OR FALSE?
Panda bears can't swim.

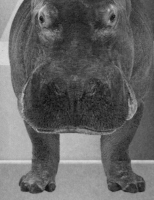

9 Which animal might you find out at night in the desert?

a. coyote
b. moose
c. leopard
d. alligator

 coyote moose

 leopard alligator

8 Hippos have red-orange _____.

a. fur
b. sweat
c. horns
d. feathers

10 How do honeybees tell each other where to find flowers?

a. with a honey trail
b. by buzzing
c. with a map
d. by dancing

11 From where does the narwhal's long, spiral horn grow?

a. tail   c. mouth
b. forehead   d. flippers

13 Which of these baby animals is often called a kit?

a. moose   c. fox
b. brown bear   d. goat

12 Which wild animal was declared extinct in 2011?

a. western black rhinoceros
b. flying squirrel
c. monarch butterfly
d. great white shark

15 ULTIMATE BRAIN BUSTER

WHAT SPECIES OF BUTTERFLY IS SHOWN HERE?

14 Which type of animal is a little red flying fox?

a. dog
b. squirrel
c. bat
d. fish

CHECK YOUR ANSWERS ON PAGES 158–159.

Globe
TROTTING

SAY WHAT!

1 True or false? In Great Britain, the **trunk** of a car is known as the "boot."

2 In total, about how many languages are spoken around the **world?**

a. 70
b. 700
c. 7,000
d. 7 million

3 What word describes someone who can speak **two** languages?

a. duolang
b. bilingual
c. trilingual
d. doublespeak

4 What is the most used **language** in the world?

a. Chinese (Mandarin)
b. Spanish
c. English
d. text message

5 **How** many letters are there in the longest word in the Merriam-Webster unabridged dictionary?

a. 189,819
b. 27
c. 45
d. 6,000,003

6 *Kummerspeck* is a German word that means _____.

a. a speck of dust in the summertime
b. weight gained when you're sad
c. a tiny bug found in kitchens
d. "Come here for a second"

7 In Scotland, if you're introducing someone but forgot their name, what is that feeling called?

a. tartle
b. humfr
c. agna
d. wazzizznaym

8 What is the world's oldest written language?

a. Egyptian
b. Sumerian from southwest Asia
c. Aztec from Mexico
d. English

9 True or false? The Iranian word *zhaghzhagh* means "a crooked path."

10 What sounds are the Khoisan languages of South Africa known for?

a. whistles
b. clicks
c. hoots
d. shouts

11 The Khmer language of Cambodia has the most letters of any alphabet. How many letters is that?

a. 27
b. 32
c. 74
d. 1,819

12 On Easter Island, what word means "borrowing everything from a friend's house"?

a. *tingo*
b. *wingo*
c. *mingo*
d. *bingo*

13 Which country has 11 official languages?

a. Russia
b. China
c. South Africa
d. U.S.A.

CHECK YOUR ANSWERS ON PAGES 159–161.

ENDS OF THE EARTH

1 On Earth, what are the polar ice caps?

a. sections in the middle of the planet covered with ice
b. sections at the top and bottom of the planet covered with ice
c. ice inside the planet
d. a cap you wear when it's cold outside

2 True or false? In the wild, polar bears and penguins are found together.

3 What has melting ice created at the North Pole?

a. a lake
b. a hurricane
c. more fish
d. unhappy Santa

4 True or false? The only animals that prey on polar bears are humans.

5 Which type of land animals are naturally found in Antarctica?

a. mammals   c. amphibians
b. reptiles   d. none

6 What is it called when an iceberg falls off of a glacier?

a. crashing
b. calving
c. slicing
d. berging

7 True or false? All glaciers are white.

8 Which of the following places on Earth do penguins not live?

a. the North Pole
b. near the equator
c. in the south, near Antarctica
d. in the zoo

9 Which of the following happens to penguins once a year?

a. have a baby
b. lose all their feathers
c. turn all white
d. sleep

10 In winter, off the coast of Antarctica, sea ice covers an area almost the size of North America. By summer's end, how much of that ice may have melted?

a. 25 percent
b. 50 percent
c. 85 percent
d. none

11 In colder weather, polar bears go out on sea ice to hunt. What do they do in warmer weather when the ice melts?

a. hibernate
b. move back on shore
c. shed their fur
d. swim

12 Where on Earth is the ice thickest?

a. the North Pole
b. the South Pole
c. Siberia
d. Alaska

13 What is the main way polar bears keep from slipping on the ice?

a. their claws dig into the ice
b. their fur melts the ice beneath them
c. rough pads on their paws create friction
d. they have excellent balance

14 Which land animal is found in the Arctic?

a. arctic fox
b. arctic hare
c. arctic wolf
d. all of the above

15 True or false?

During the summer, the sun never sets at the North and South Poles.

There's No Place LIKE HOME

PALACE OF VERSAILLES

① Who was the first president to live in the White House?
a. George Washington
b. John Adams
c. James Monroe
d. John F. Kennedy

② **True or false?** At the Palace of Versailles in France, King Louis XVI installed a chimney invented by Benjamin Franklin.

③ Buckingham Palace in London is where the Queen of England lives. What was there before the palace was built?
a. a mulberry-bush garden for silkworms
b. a shoe factory for the British army
c. a Viking castle
d. a small house where the Buckingham family lived

BUCKINGHAM PALACE ROAD SW1
CITY OF WESTMINSTER

④ Where does the Pope live?
a. Notre-Dame Cathedral   c. the Vatican
b. Westminster Abbey   d. suburbs of Rome, Italy

⑤ Why did people thousands of years ago build cave houses and underground cities in the rocks of Cappadocia, Turkey?
a. it is very cold there
b. to hide from attackers
c. to hide from animals
d. to create a tourist spot

⑥ What is especially crazy about the "Crazy House" in Bispingen, Germany?
a. it has no doors
b. it has no roof
c. it is upside down
d. it floats

CAPPADOCIA CAVE HOUSES

7 The fictional detective Sherlock Holmes lives at 221B Baker Street in which city?

a. Paris, France   **c.** Boston, Massachusetts
b. London, England   **d.** Tokyo, Japan

8 The house in the picture below belongs to which author of great American children's novels?

a. J.K. Rowling
b. Mark Twain
c. Dr. Seuss
d. William Shakespeare

BRAN CASTLE

9 In what country is Bran Castle, also known as "Dracula's Castle"?

a. Romania
b. England
c. France
d. Bulgaria

10 **True or false?** A man in Poland built the world's skinniest house. It's 3 feet (0.9 m) wide at its narrowest point, and 5 feet (1.5 m) at its widest.

11 The 27-story "Antilia" in Mumbai, India, is the world's most expensive home. How much did it cost to build?

a. $10 million
b. $100 million
c. $1 billion
d. $1 million

12 **True or false?** A baker in Switzerland built a house that looks like a chocolate-frosted donut.

What's for DINNER?

NOODLES

1 **True or false?** People in 80 percent of the world's countries eat insects.

2 **In Japan, what is the polite way to eat noodles?**
a. with a fork
b. very quietly
c. slurp them
d. one at a time

3 **If you were served *hákarl* in Iceland, what would you be eating?**
a. clear Jell-O
b. spicy ice cream
c. rotten shark
d. chocolate French fries

4 **In Chile, it is bad manners to touch your food with this.**
a. a fork
b. a knife
c. your hands
d. the menu

ROOSTER

5 **The red thing on top of a rooster's head is used in Italy as an ingredient to make _____.**
a. a stew
b. a sauce
c. a sandwich
d. gummy bears

6 **True or false?** Most people in India eat using only their left hand.

7 In Korea, what is the dish *sannakji*?

a. live octopus
b. see-through bread
c. blue steak
d. breakfast cereal

8 In Russia, where is the polite place to rest your wrists during a meal?

a. in your lap
b. on the edge of the table
c. on your plate
d. in a toy bed next to your napkin

BREAD

9 If you accidentally drop bread on the floor during a meal in Afghanistan, what should you do?

a. leave it there
b. pick it up, kiss it, and touch it to your forehead
c. eat it before five seconds pass
d. kick it across the room

10 Besides the spiky outside, what is most noticeable about the durian fruit from Southeast Asia?

a. terrible odor
b. very sour taste
c. explodes when ripe
d. attracts monkeys

DURIAN FRUIT

11 In Bahrain, what do you do to show you enjoyed a meal?

a. sing
b. burp
c. applaud
d. sneeze

12 The English translation of a popular Chinese dish is "saliva chicken." Why is it called this?

a. contains saliva from a chicken
b. contains saliva from the chef
c. so good it makes your mouth water
d. so bad you spit it out

13 True or false? In Ethiopia, a family normally shares one large plate during a meal.

CHECK YOUR ANSWERS ON PAGES 159–161.

TRUE or FALSE?
Where in the World?

1. IRAN AND THE U.S.A. ARE THE WORLD'S TWO BIGGEST GROWERS OF PISTACHIO NUTS.

2. THE GREAT WALL OF CHINA COULD SURROUND THE ENTIRE COUNTRY OF AUSTRALIA.

3. THE WORLD'S RICHEST COUNTRY IS QATAR.

4. THE HIGHEST TEMPERATURE EVER RECORDED, 134°F (56.7°C), WAS IN LIBYA.

5. THE LOWEST TEMPERATURE EVER RECORDED, −128.5°F (−89.2°C), WAS IN ANTARCTICA.

6. IN THE NETHERLANDS, THERE ARE THREE TIMES AS MANY BIKES AS CARS.

7. THE AMAZON RIVER IN SOUTH AMERICA IS THE LONGEST RIVER IN THE WORLD.

8. ONLY ABOUT 50 PEOPLE LIVE ON THE PITCAIRN ISLANDS, A BRITISH OVERSEAS TERRITORY IN THE SOUTH PACIFIC OCEAN.

9. FOSSILS OF HUMANS' EARLIEST ANCESTORS HAVE BEEN FOUND IN NEW ZEALAND.

10. MOUNT KOSCIUSZKO, THE HIGHEST MOUNTAIN IN AUSTRALIA, IS NAMED AFTER A MAN FROM POLAND.

11. URUGUAY HAS WON THE SOCCER WORLD CUP CHAMPIONSHIP MORE TIMES THAN ANY OTHER COUNTRY.

12. A TYPICAL GREETING IN INDONESIA IS *APA KHABAR.*

13. THERE ARE MORE LAKES IN CANADA THAN IN ALL OTHER COUNTRIES COMBINED.

14. HORSEBACK RIDING IS THE NUMBER ONE SPORT FOR BOTH BOYS AND GIRLS IN SWEDEN.

15. THAILAND IS THE WORLD'S BIGGEST PRODUCER OF TIN.

16 IN ICELAND'S PHONE DIRECTORIES, YOU ARE LISTED BY YOUR FIRST NAME INSTEAD OF YOUR LAST NAME.

17 HALF OF THE CORK IN THE WORLD COMES FROM PORTUGAL.

18 THE MONEY IN BOTSWANA IS CALLED *PULA*, WHICH MEANS "SUNSHINE."

19 IT IS A TRADITION IN PERU TO WEAR YELLOW UNDERWEAR ON NEW YEAR'S EVE.

20 THE TURKEY IS THE NATIONAL BIRD OF TURKEY.

21 EVERY YEAR IN SOUTH KOREA THERE IS A BIG FESTIVAL WHERE PEOPLE PLAY IN THE MUD.

22 THE SAXOPHONE WAS INVENTED IN BELGIUM BY A MAN NAMED ADOLPHE SAX.

23 CHILE WAS THE FIRST COUNTRY TO HAVE A FEMALE PRESIDENT.

24 IN A MUSEUM IN UKRAINE, THERE IS A FLEA WEARING GOLDEN HORSESHOES.

25 THE FIRST FULL-LENGTH ANIMATED MOVIE WAS MADE IN ARGENTINA.

26 HOLDING UP A CLOSED FIST IS AN INSULT IN GREECE.

27 MOUNTAIN CLIMBING IS THE NATIONAL SPORT OF DENMARK.

28 THE BOBO PEOPLE OF BURKINA FASO ARE KNOWN FOR MAKING LARGE BUTTERFLY MASKS.

29 NEPAL IS THE ONLY COUNTRY WITH A FLAG THAT'S NOT RECTANGULAR.

30 IN GUATEMALA, CHILDREN LEAVE THEIR BABY TEETH FOR A MAGIC CAT CALLED EL GATO INSTEAD OF THE TOOTH FAIRY.

CHECK YOUR ANSWERS ON PAGES 159–161.

Lucky CHARMS

1 From Ireland we get the lucky four-leaf clover. What do the leaves stand for?

a. north, south, east, and west
b. faith, hope, love, and luck
c. birth, childhood, adulthood, and death
d. eeny, meeny, miney, and moe

2 **True or false?** In some Scandinavian countries, people think placing an acorn on their windowsill will keep away lightning.

3 In Japan, what does it mean if you see a Daruma doll with only one eye painted in?

a. the owner made a wish that hasn't yet come true
b. the doll is keeping one eye open for evil spirits
c. the owner can make another wish
d. the owner ran out of paint

4 A common Egyptian charm is the scarab. What is it in the shape of?

a. an eye   c. a flower
b. a beetle   d. a sacred crab

5 In Chinese culture, which little creature is a symbol of good luck?

a. cricket   c. ant
b. spider   d. firefly

DARUMA DOLL

NAZAR BLUE EYE CHARM

6 **True or false?** Some people in South Africa think vulture heads are good luck and help see the future.

7 **True or false?** The Nazar blue eye charm, which is said to keep away evil, is very popular in Spain.

8 In Austria, why do they say a coin is lucky if you find it during a rainstorm?

a. it fell from heaven
b. it will stop raining within 5 hours
c. it will clean away troubles
d. it took your mind away from getting wet

9 Horseshoes are considered lucky in the United Kingdom, the U.S.A., and elsewhere. Some people say that to be lucky, _____.

a. the ends of the horseshoe must be facing up
b. the ends must be facing down
c. the ends can either face up or down
d. all of the above

10 **True or false?** Native people in Australia believe that frogs are a good luck charm that help plants grow.

AUSTRALIAN GREEN TREE FROG

CHECK YOUR ANSWERS ON PAGES 159–161.

BACK TO SCHOOL

1 True or false? In South Africa, before entering school, children form **two lines:** one for boys and one for girls.

2 In which **city** was the first public school in the United States?

a. Philadelphia, Pennsylvania
b. Boston, Massachusetts
c. Dallas, Texas
d. South Bend, Indiana

3 True or false? On the first day of 1st grade in Germany, students are given a *Schultuete*—a colorful hat.

4 In Australia, where the sun can be very hot, what are kids required to **wear** during recess?

a. hats
b. short-sleeved shirts
c. sunscreen
d. clip-on fans

5 The **tradition** of giving an apple to the teacher started in Denmark and Sweden. **Why?**

a. they were the apple capitals of the world
b. the apple was part of the teacher's payment
c. apples were considered lucky
d. teachers gave extra credit for fruit

6 When a teacher in Japan is talking to a student who has misbehaved, what must the **student** do?

a. look the teacher in the eye
b. look at the floor
c. close their eyes
d. cover their eyes with their hands

7 In Finland, kids in elementary school get about **75** minutes of recess a day. About how long is recess in the U.S.A.?

a. 60 minutes   c. 27 minutes
b. 45 minutes   d. 15 minutes

8 True or false? In Britain, students are required to sit down as soon as the teacher enters the **classroom.**

9 Where was the unique location of a science school in Dongzhong, China?

a. in a tree   c. in a cave
b. at the top of a   d. in a school bus
   skyscraper

10 In the U.S.A., the school year is 180 days long. How long is it in **Indonesia?**

a. 150 days   c. 244 days
b. 180 days   d. 365 days

11 The world's biggest school is in Lucknow, India. About how many **students** attend?

a. 5,500   c. 32,000
b. 12,000   d. 108,000

12 In France, there is traditionally **no** school on ____.

a. Wednesdays
b. Napoleon's birthday
c. the first day of winter
d. dates with prime numbers

13 In 1994, the United Nations declared a World Teachers' Day. On what date is it celebrated each year?

a. September 1   c. December 20
b. October 5   d. June 25

14 True or false? As a result of frequent flooding in Bangladesh, some students go to school on a **boat.**

MAP MANIA!
ROADSIDE ATTRACTIONS

① BANGKOK, THAILAND

With a giant dragon spiraling to its roof, what is the Wat Samphran building?

a. an apartment building
b. an amusement park
c. a museum
d. a temple

② SOFIA, BULGARIA

Architect Simeon Simeonov built a house shaped like a giant snail to encourage people to live more "green" lifestyles. What are the radiator heaters inside in the shape of?

a. frogs
b. ladybugs
c. pumpkins
d. all of the above

ATLANTIC OCEAN

SOUTH AMERICA

PACIFIC OCEAN

④ BATHURST, SOUTH AFRICA

Why is there a Big Pineapple in this little town?

a. it was the first crop to grow in the area
b. the town is located in Pineapple County
c. the world's largest pineapple was grown here
d. they meant to build a big pine cone and never fixed it

③ BOM PRINCÍPIO, BRAZIL

What is the giant strawberry-shaped building in this town?

a. home of the owner of a produce stand
b. entrance to the National Strawberry Festival
c. café specializing in strawberry shortcake
d. toy store

5. COOMBS, CANADA

A family of goats lives on the roof of the Old Country Market during the summer! Kristian Graaten, the original owner, put grass on the roof in the style of buildings from his home country. What country is that?

a. Norway
b. Germany
c. Australia
d. Cuba

6. TAMWORTH, AUSTRALIA

The Big Golden Guitar is a giant version of the trophy from Australia's Country Music Awards. About how tall is this guitar?

a. 12 feet (3.7 m)
b. 39 feet (11.9 m)
c. 76 feet (23.2 m)
d. 300 feet (91.4 m)

ARCTIC OCEAN

EUROPE

ASIA

D

AFRICA

F

PACIFIC OCEAN

INDIAN OCEAN

AUSTRALIA

G

E

8–14

MATCH EACH OF THESE ATTRACTIONS TO THE RED DOT THAT SHOWS ITS CORRECT LOCATION ON THE MAP.

7. AMARILLO, TEXAS

Cadillac Ranch is a famous art display. There are ten Cadillac cars in a row, halfway buried in the dirt nose-first. Why were the cars placed at an angle?

a. to match the angle of the Cadillac factory entrance in Detroit, Michigan
b. to match the angle of a famous old restaurant sign in the town
c. to be at the same angle as the Great Pyramid of Giza in Egypt
d. to reflect sunlight, creating a cool light show

GAME SHOW

ULTIMATE GLOBAL CHALLENGE

1 In which country do students take their shoes off before entering the classroom?
a. Japan
b. Switzerland
c. Cuba
d. Czech Republic

2
TRUE OR FALSE?
The ice caps at the North and South Poles melt during the same months.

3 The castle pictured below, in Darmstadt, Germany, shares its name with what fictional character?
a. The Count of Monte Cristo
b. Dumbledore
c. Frankenstein
d. Tinkerbell

4 When eating in Thailand, when do you use your fork?
a. only to push food onto your spoon
b. only when you can't use chopsticks
c. only to eat meat, not noodles
d. only in the evening

5 TRUE OR FALSE?
The guinea pig was originally found in Guinea, Africa.

6 In which country does this animal's name—*fu*—mean "good luck"?
a. Pakistan
b. Suriname
c. China
d. Dominican Republic

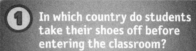

7 How would you say "hello" to someone who speaks Breton in Brittany, France?
a. *Bonjour*
b. *Degemer mad*
c. *Dobar dan*
d. *Hello*

8 In what country will you find the world's largest sundial, an instrument used to tell the time?

a. Australia c. Russia
b. India d. U.S.A.

9 If you went to England and got on an elevator, you would actually call it _____.

a. a lorry c. a puller
b. a lift d. an escalator

10 What is the main food for the animal pictured below?
a. fish
b. birds
c. seals
d. foxes

11 In Portugal, the house pictured below is known as what?
a. House of Mud
b. House of Pebbles
c. House of Stone
d. House of Pancakes

12 TRUE OR FALSE?

In Afghanistan, guests at a meal are seated the farthest away from the door.

13 In Ukraine, a *pysanka* is a symbol of good luck. What does the pysanka look like?
a. four-leaf clover
b. chicken
c. Easter egg
d. rabbit's foot

14 What is the official name of Luxembourg?

a. the People's Republic of Luxembourg
b. the Principality of Luxembourg
c. the Commonwealth of Luxembourg
d. the Grand Duchy of Luxembourg

15 ULTIMATE BRAIN BUSTER

THE "WORLD'S LARGEST" OF ONE OF THE FOLLOWING IS LOCATED IN NEWARK, OHIO, U.S.A. WHICH ONE IS IT?

a.
picnic basket

b.
banana

c.
rubber duck

d.
boot

CHECK YOUR ANSWERS ON PAGES 159–161.

DID YOU KNOW? THE STORIES OF THE HOBBIT BILBO BAGGINS AND HIS COUSIN FRODO, IN THE LORD OF THE RINGS SERIES, ARE BASED ON SCANDINAVIAN AND ANGLO-SAXON SAGAS MORE THAN 1,500 YEARS OLD.

Pop CULTURE

THE HOBBIT :
AN UNEXPECTED JOURNEY

Channel SURFING

1 Which underwater city does SpongeBob SquarePants call home?

a. Sandy Shores **c.** Shell City
b. Bikini Bottom **d.** Tentacle Acres

2 True or false?

The blog See Stan Blog is written by a dog.

3 Which of the following singers was not an *American Idol* winner?

a. Kelly Clarkson
b. Carrie Underwood
c. Phillip Phillips
d. Danielle Bradbury

4 The Pritchett and Dunphy families appear on what show?

a. *Teenage Mutant Ninja Turtles* **c.** *Modern Family*
b. *Phineas and Ferb* **d.** *The Goldbergs*

5 Which food was served at Charlie Brown's Thanksgiving dinner?

a. turkey and stuffing
b. toast and popcorn
c. bacon and eggs
d. veggie burgers and salad

6 Which of the following talent shows has Simon Cowell *not* judged?

a. *The X-Factor* **c.** *American Idol*
b. *America's Got Talent* **d.** *Britain's Got Talent*

SIMON COWELL

Pop CULTURE

7 Which of the following shows is *not* based on a popular movie?

a. *Sanjay and Craig*
b. *The Penguins of Madagascar*
c. *Kung Fu Panda: Legends of Awesomeness*
d. *Monsters vs. Aliens*

8 What do the letters T.U.F.F. in *T.U.F.F. Puppy* stand for?

a. Tough Until Freaky Friday
b. Turbo Undercover Fighting Force
c. Tough Unstoppable Fighting Felines
d. Tomatoes Udon Figs Fajitas

9 *Sam & Cat* is a spinoff of which two shows?

a. *iCarly* and *Victorious*
b. *Good Luck Charlie* and *Victorious*
c. *The Simpsons* and *The Fairly OddParents*
d. *T.U.F.F. Puppy* and *A.N.T. Farm*

10 On the TV show *Jessie*, the family Jessie nannies for has a pet named Mr. Kipling. What type of animal is he?

a. cat
b. parrot
c. hamster
d. monitor lizard

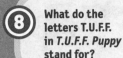

LISA
SIMPSON

11 What instrument does Lisa Simpson play?

a. clarinet
b. drums
c. piano
d. saxophone

12 What fictional planet is WordGirl from?

a. Krypton
b. Lexicon
c. Galacticon
d. Emoticon

13 True or false?

The members of One Direction were discovered on the show *The X-Factor*.

ONE DIRECTION

SUPER SIDEKICKS

1 Sam the Hobbit protects his best friend, Frodo, on a mission to _____.
a. find Middle-earth
b. destroy a powerful ring
c. capture the Dark Lord Sauron
d. defeat a wizard named Gandalf

2 When Mermaid Man needs assistance protecting Bikini Bottom, whom does he rely on?
a. Barnacle Boy
b. Aquaman
c. Neptune
d. Ariel

3 What causes a brief rift between Megamind and Minion?
a. Megamind develops a crush on Roxanne
b. Megamind destroys Metro Man
c. Minion wants to be a hero instead of a villain
d. a museum is named after Megamind instead of Minion

4 Which shifty sidekick has been linked to both Magneto and Professor Xavier?
a. Rogue
b. Storm
c. Jean Gray
d. Mystique

5 Which of Tony Stark's sidekicks wears an Iron Patriot suit in *Iron Man 3*?
a. James "Rhodey" Rhodes
b. Pepper Potts
c. Harley Keener
d. Nick Fury

6 Bucky Barnes can often be found fighting alongside which superhero?
a. Batman
b. Spider-Man
c. Captain America
d. Hulk

7 Which of the following is a nickname for Batman's sidekick, Robin?
a. The Caped Crusader
b. Man of Steel
c. Boy Wonder
d. Spidey

8 Han Solo's pal Chewbacca is what type of creature?
a. Wookiee
b. Clone
c. Ewok
d. Hutt

9 The first name of supersleuth Dr. Watson is _____.
a. Sherlock
b. John
c. Cornelius
d. Larry

10 Which of the following is Shrek the ogre's best friend?
a. Gingerbread Man
b. Donkey
c. Lord Farquaad
d. Pinocchio

SUPERMAN

11 When Superman isn't leaping tall buildings, he works with Jimmy Olsen at which newspaper?
a. *Washington Post*
b. *San Francisco Chronicle*
c. *Daily Planet*
d. *Dallas Star*

12 Kato's high-flying kicks have often saved which hero?
a. Green Lantern
b. Green Hornet
c. Green Goblin
d. Green Arrow

13 Which of Harry Potter's sidekicks has parents who are Muggles?
a. Hermione Granger
b. Ron Weasley
c. Luna Lovegood
d. Tom Riddle

TRUE or FALSE?
It's Showtime!

1 IN *MUPPETS MOST WANTED*, CONSTANTINE PRETENDS TO BE KERMIT THE FROG.

2 THE MADAGASCAR MOVIES HAVE TAKEN PLACE ON EVERY CONTINENT IN THE WORLD.

3 IN *MEN IN BLACK 3*, AGENT J TEAMS UP WITH A YOUNGER VERSION OF AGENT K.

4 IN THE MOVIE *BRAVE*, KING FERGUS GIVES MERIDA A SET OF BOW AND ARROWS FOR HER BIRTHDAY.

5 IN *THOR: THE DARK WORLD*, LOKI MORPHS INTO THE HULK.

6 IT'S REVEALED IN *THE SMURFS 2* THAT GARGAMEL CREATED THE SMURFS.

7 WRECK-IT RALPH IS THE VILLAIN OF A VIDEO GAME CALLED *WRECK-IT RALPH*.

8 *HOTEL TRANSYLVANIA* TAKES PLACE ON MAVIS'S 18TH BIRTHDAY.

9 MALEFICENT CASTS A SLEEPING SPELL ON SNOW WHITE.

10 IN *THE AMAZING SPIDER-MAN*, GWEN STACY'S FATHER IS THE SCHOOL PRINCIPAL.

11 THE LONE RANGER'S SIDEKICK, TONTO, IS A MEMBER OF THE NAVAJO INDIAN TRIBE.

12 IN *MEGAMIND*, METRO MAN CLAIMS THAT COPPER DRAINS HIS POWERS.

13 SONIC THE HEDGEHOG MAKES AN APPEARANCE IN THE MOVIE *WRECK-IT RALPH*.

14 INDIANA JONES HAS OPHIDIOPHOBIA, OR A FEAR OF SNAKES.

15 IN *THE LEGO MOVIE*, LORD BUSINESS PLANS TO DESTROY THE WORLD BY GLUING IT TOGETHER.

Pop CULTURE

16 PERCY JACKSON MUST STEAL ZEUS'S LIGHTNING BOLT IN *PERCY JACKSON: SEA OF MONSTERS*.

17 IN *DESPICABLE ME 2*, GRU WORKS IN A BAKERY AT A MALL.

18 ROAR OMEGA ROAR IS A FRATERNITY FOR MISFIT MONSTERS IN *MONSTERS UNIVERSITY*.

19 IN *MAN OF STEEL*, SUPERMAN BATTLES VILLAIN LEX LUTHOR.

20 *THE HOBBIT: AN UNEXPECTED JOURNEY* TELLS THE STORY OF A HOBBIT NAMED FRODO.

21 CHEESPIDERS, MISQUITOASTS, AND SHRIMPANZEES ARE CREATURES CALLED FOODIMALS IN *CLOUDY WITH A CHANCE OF MEATBALLS 2*.

22 *JOURNEY 2: THE MYSTERIOUS ISLAND* WAS INSPIRED BY A NOVEL BY JULES VERNE.

23 KATNISS EVERDEEN AND PEETA MELLARK ARE THE ONLY DISTRICT 12 RESIDENTS TO HAVE EVER WON THE HUNGER GAMES.

24 MOST OF *THE WOLVERINE* TAKES PLACE IN JAPAN.

25 IN THE MOVIE *FROZEN*, ELSA IS BORN WITH THE POWER TO MAKE SNOW AND ICE.

26 IN THE MOVIE *ENDER'S GAME*, ENDER IS GIVEN COMMAND OF DRAGON ARMY.

27 *MR. PEABODY & SHERMAN* TELLS THE STORY OF A DOG AND HIS PET BOY.

28 IN *SHREK FOREVER AFTER*, RUMPELSTILTSKIN SEEKS REVENGE ON SHREK FOR RUINING HIS CHANCES OF BECOMING KING.

29 DR. BRUCE BANNER, WHO APPEARS IN *THE AVENGERS*, IS THE DIRECTOR OF S.H.I.E.L.D.

30 IN *OZ THE GREAT AND POWERFUL*, THEODORA TURNS INTO A GREEN-SKINNED WITCH AFTER EATING A PINEAPPLE.

CHECK YOUR ANSWERS ON PAGES 161–162.

All in the FAMILY

VENUS AND SERENA WILLIAMS

① On which television show have tennis superstars Venus and Serena Williams appeared as animation characters?

a. *The Simpsons*
b. *Max Steel*
c. *Dora the Explorer*
d. *Monsters vs. Aliens*

② Which of the following residences is home to the British royal family?

a. Neuschwanstein Castle
b. Palace of Versailles
c. Hogwarts
d. Buckingham Palace

THE BRITISH ROYAL FAMILY

③ True or false? Two of the members of the band the Wanted are brothers.

④ Which of the following movies has not starred any of the Hemsworth brothers?

a. *Thor: The Dark World*
b. *The Hunger Games: Catching Fire*
c. *X-Men: First Class*
d. *Snow White & the Huntsman*

⑤ The sister of this celebrity had a hit song called "Whip My Hair."

a. Jaden Smith
b. Selena Gomez
c. Bruno Mars
d. Katy Perry

⑥ Derek and Julianne Hough are best known for which of the following activities?

a. gymnastics
b. dancing
c. cooking
d. fashion design

7 Which of the following expressions would you most likely associate with the Molina brothers?

a. Batter up!
b. Touchdown!
c. Goal!
d. Put your pencils down!

8 In 2013, the Obamas welcomed a new dog named Sunny to the family. Which breed was the new pup?

a. Portuguese water dog
b. Brussels griffon
c. Boston terrier
d. Shar-Pei

9 Which famous country music group is a family act?

a. Lady Antebellum
b. The Band Perry
c. Little Big Town
d. Florida Georgia Line

10 Which of the following objects would the Ingalls family never have used in their home on the prairie?

a. a horse and buggy
b. a television
c. a hammer
d. a frying pan

11 True or false?
The twins on the TV show *Liv and Maddie* are portrayed by real twin sisters.

12 Which of the following brothers each owns a Super Bowl ring?

a. Jason and Devin McCourty
b. Eli and Peyton Manning
c. José and Yadier Molina
d. Chad and Keyshawn Johnson

13 Emma Roberts's famous aunt, Julia Roberts, played which character in the movie *Mirror Mirror*?

a. Snow White
b. Queen Clementianna
c. Magic Mirror
d. Chuckles

FOOTBALL

GAME CENTRAL

1 In *Plants vs. Zombies*, how do the **zombies** warn players of an attack?

a. they send flowers
b. they write a letter
c. they send a text message
d. there is no warning

2 Which of the following is **not** an Angry Birds game?

a. *Angry Birds Rio*
b. *Angry Birds Space*
c. *Angry Birds Seasons*
d. *Angry Birds Star Trek*

3 Which character does *not* appear in *Lego Marvel* **Super Heroes**?

a. Batman
b. Iron Man
c. Hulk
d. Spider-Man

4 In the game *Fruit Ninja*, which of the following should you avoid slicing?

a. dragon fruit
b. bomb
c. any vegetable
d. watermelon

5 In the **survival** mode of *Minecraft*, players must protect themselves from ____.

a. monsters
b. ghosts
c. miners
d. birds

6 Which character can you **buy** furniture from in *Animal Crossing*?

a. Ganon
b. Tom Nook
c. Dr. Eggman
d. Link

7 Which character **does not** appear in *Disney Infinity*?

a. Captain Jack Sparrow
b. Mr. Incredible
c. Patrick Starfish
d. Mickey Mouse

8 The **action** in the classic video game *Frogger* is to ____.

a. hop across lily pads
b. eat many flies
c. battle alien robots
d. cross the street while avoiding cars

9 What playground term is used to describe video games that allow a player to build things?

a. sandbox   c. slide
b. jungle gym   d. seesaw

10 Which artist's music does not appear in *Just Dance 2014*?

a. Taylor Swift   c. PSY
b. One Direction   d. Katy Perry

11 As of 2013, what is the top-selling video game of all time?

a. *Pac-Man*   c. *Wii Sports*
b. *Super Mario Bros.*   d. *Sonic the Hedgehog*

12 In what **country** does *Temple Run: Brave* take place?

a. Turkey
b. Argentina
c. Egypt
d. Scotland

13 What is Mario and Luigi's job?

a. plumber   c. zookeeper
b. doctor   d. pizza maker

14 **Tree Rex,** Bouncer, and Swarm are characters from which video game?

a. *Pokémon X*
b. *Disney Infinity*
c. *Skylanders: Giants*
d. *Barbie Dreamhouse Party*

CHECK YOUR ANSWERS ON PAGES 161–162.

GAME SHOW

ULTIMATE POP CULTURE CHALLENGE

1 In which of the following video games would you expect to find Mario Balotelli?

a. *Grand Slam Tennis 2*
b. *Madden NFL 25*
c. *FIFA 14*
d. *NHL 14*

2 What is the relationship between Greg and Rowley in the Diary of a Wimpy Kid series?

a. brothers
b. cousins
c. friends
d. teacher and student

3 In the series finale of *Wizards of Waverly Place*, the name of the family wizard was finally revealed. Who was it?

a. Alex Russo
b. Max Russo
c. Justin Russo
d. Jerry Russo

4 **TRUE OR FALSE?**

In the book *The Wonderful Wizard of Oz* by L. Frank Baum, Dorothy's slippers are ruby.

5 What do all winners of Nickelodeon Kids' Choice Awards receive?

a. slime
b. a blimp
c. a surfboard
d. a moon man

6 Match the supervillain to the book he or she appears in.

a. The White Witch
b. Shere Khan
c. Lord Voldemort
d. Cruella de Vil

e. *The Jungle Book*
f. *The Hundred and One Dalmatians*
g. *Harry Potter and the Deathly Hallows*
h. *The Lion, the Witch, and the Wardrobe*

Pop CULTURE

7 Which famous 1990s boy band was Justin Timberlake a member of before going solo?
a. Backstreet Boys
b. New Kids on the Block
c. Boys II Men
d. 'N Sync

8 In which country did anime originate?
a. China
b. Japan
c. South Korea
d. India

9 What is Internet sensation Grumpy Cat's real name?
a. Sourpuss
b. Tardar Sauce
c. Socks
d. Colonel Meow

10 Which artist has judged every season of *The Voice* in the United States?
a. Adam Levine
b. CeeLo Green
c. Christina Aguilera
d. Usher

11 Which of these popular words was named "word of the year" by Oxford Dictionaries in 2013?
a. selfie
b. hashtag
c. photobomb
d. tweet

12 "More than meets the eye" is a tagline for what series?
a. *X-Men*
b. *Toy Story*
c. *Transformers*
d. *Spider-Man*

13 Match these Ice Age characters to the movie in the series in which they appeared.
a. Human baby
b. Captain Gutt
c. Crash
d. Scratte
e. *Ice Age: Continental Drift*
f. *Ice Age: The Meltdown*
g. *Ice Age: Dawn of the Dinosaurs*
h. *Ice Age*

14 ULTIMATE BRAIN BUSTER
WHICH OF THESE ARTISTS PERFORMED AT THE SUPER BOWL HALF-TIME SHOW IN 2014?

a. Beyoncé
b. Bruno Mars
c. Carly Rae Jepsen
d. P!nk

CHECK YOUR ANSWERS ON PAGES 161–162.

Natural
WONDERS

IS EVERYONE DRESSED UP FOR A NIGHT ON THE REEF?

TROPICAL CORAL REEF

Great BARRIER REEF

THE GREAT BARRIER REEF

1 **True or false?**
The coral that makes up the Great Barrier Reef is a kind of rock.

2 The giant clam can reach 4 feet (1.2 m) in length and can weigh as much as _____ .

a. 10 pounds (4.5 kg)
b. 50 pounds (22.7 kg)
c. 100 pounds (45.4 kg)
d. 500 pounds (226.8 kg)

GIANT CLAM

3 **True or false?**
Astronauts can see the Great Barrier Reef from space.

4 What is this type of coral called?

a. dome coral
b. squiggly coral
c. brain coral
d. maze coral

5 What do corals eat?

a. algae
b. clownfish
c. hamburgers
d. they're not alive

6 Which reef creature can poison a person to death?

a. cone snail
b. stingray
c. box jellyfish
d. all of the above

CROWN-OF-THORNS STARFISH

7 What does a crown-of-thorns starfish do to coral in order to eat it?

a. injects poison into it
b. spreads its stomach over it
c. sprinkles salt and pepper on it
d. nothing can eat coral

8 The 1,430-mile (2,300-km)-long Great Barrier Reef would fit inside of the U.S. state of _____.

a. Florida
b. Alaska
c. Nebraska
d. Oregon

9 Which of the following threatens the existence of the Great Barrier Reef?

a. climate change
b. the crown-of-thorns starfish
c. tourists
d. all of the above

10 Where do green sea turtles live?

a. in oceans around the world
b. in lakes in Australia
c. in swamps and marshes
d. on the moon

11 What is the name of this fish that lives in the Great Barrier Reef?

a. rainbow fish
b. spinefoot fish
c. lionfish
d. parrotfish

12 True or false? Cuttlefish are not actually fish.

CUTTLEFISH

FORCES OF NATURE

1 What is a **large, rotating thunderstorm** called?

a. supercell
b. spin doctor
c. lightning ball
d. tilt-a-whirl

2 Which **natural disaster** destroyed a nuclear power plant in **Japan** in 2011?

a. hurricane
b. tornado
c. tsunami
d. volcano

3 Which of the following does not trigger an **avalanche?**

a. skiing down a mountain
b. shouting loudly
c. heavy wind
d. a sudden change in temperature

4 Which force of nature kills the most **people** each year on average?

a. extreme heat
b. tornadoes
c. lightning
d. floods

5 True or false? A sinkhole can swallow up an entire building.

6 Where was the **biggest** dust storm scientists have ever seen?

a. Mars
b. China
c. the Sahara
d. Nebraska

7 What can happen when an **airplane** flies through ash from a **volcanic** eruption?

a. the entire plane melts
b. the engines stop
c. the people inside get coated in dust
d. all of the above

8 What does a **seismograph** measure?

a. the size of a hail ball
b. the strength of an earthquake
c. the depth of a flood
d. the color of quicksand

9 Dust storms are common in places with **dry weather** and what other feature?

a. vast grasslands
b. mountains
c. orange trees
d. very few plants

10 True or false? The top speed of a Chevrolet Avalanche truck is faster than the **top speed** of a snow avalanche.

11 If people cut down all of the trees on a mountain slope, which of the following may **happen**?

a. ice storm
b. forest fire
c. landslide
d. meteor strike

13 In which country do most of the tornadoes on **Earth** occur?

a. South Africa
b. Brazil
c. the United States
d. Canada

12 True or false? Scientists can predict earthquakes a week before they happen.

15 If a **tsunami**, a giant tidal wave, is traveling across the ocean at top speed, which of the following would match its pace?

a. a jet airplane
b. a cheetah
c. a speeding bullet
d. lightning

14 What is the best way to escape from **quicksand**?

a. get a friend to pull you out
b. wiggle your legs around
c. wait for it to rain
d. there's no way to escape

CHECK YOUR ANSWERS ON PAGES 163–164.

Life in EXTREMES

SONORAN DESERT TOAD

1. What do you call creatures that live in extremely harsh conditions?
- **a.** super bugs
- **b.** extremophiles
- **c.** tough cookies
- **d.** powermites

2. How do Sonoran Desert toads survive about 9 months of the year without regular access to water?
- **a.** by gathering food for the dry season
- **b.** by soaking up moisture from the air
- **c.** by hiding in an underground burrow
- **d.** by hopping all the way to the ocean

3. The black anglerfish lives in the deep ocean. What does it have growing from its head to help it attract prey?
- **a.** a glowing lure
- **b.** spiky horns
- **c.** tentacles
- **d.** an iPod

4. NASA's Curiosity rover is exploring and looking for signs of life on which planet?
- a. Venus
- b. Mars
- c. Saturn
- d. Uranus

CURIOSITY ROVER

5. True or false?
The colorful bands in this hot spring are actually colonies of bacteria.

6. Where can you find extreme bacteria hanging out in formations called snottites?
- **a.** in your nose
- **b.** in ocean trenches
- **c.** in volcanoes
- **d.** in caves

HOT SPRING

7 **True or false?**
Bactrian camels in the Gobi desert in Asia eat snow to get enough water.

8 The olm, a cave-dwelling salamander of southern Europe, doesn't have _____.
a. eyes c. a brain
b. legs d. toes

9 **True or false?**
Ostriches swallow rocks to help digest food.

BACTRIAN
CAMEL

OSTRICH

10 To keep cool in scorching-hot temperatures, kangaroos
_____.
a. lick themselves
b. dig tunnels underground
c. come out only at night
d. jump into the ocean

11 **True or false?**
Scientists have discovered life beneath the icy surface of Saturn's moon Enceladus.

12 Russian scientists who drilled through 2.3 miles (3.7 km) of ice covering Lake Vostok in Antarctica claim that they found evidence of _____.
a. aliens c. worms and shrimps
b. ancient penguins d. sharks and whales

CHECK YOUR ANSWERS ON PAGES 163–164.

STARRY SKIES

1 **What is the constellation Gemini supposed to look like?**

a. blue jeans
b. swans
c. wrestling hippos
d. twins

2 **Stars are being born in the Orion Nebula. It looks like** _____ .

a. a rocket ship
b. a strangely shaped cloud
c. empty black space
d. a little green person with big eyes

3 **True or false? All of the stars in the sky are the same distance from Earth.**

4 **If you walk toward Polaris, the Pole Star, what direction are you going?**

a. north
b. east
c. south
d. in circles

5 **What is another name for the cluster of bright stars called the Pleiades?**

a. the Blue Bubble
b. the Seven Sisters
c. the Ping-Pong People
d. the Million Marble

6 **The constellation Cassiopeia looks like the letter _W_ on its side. According to Greek mythology, it represents a** _____ .

a. hunting tiger
b. queen on her throne
c. pirate ship
d. gigantic spider

7 **What country does the oldest surviving paper map of the stars come from?**

a. England
b. France
c. China
d. India

8 Which **Zodiac** constellation represents a lion?

a. Aries
b. Virgo
c. Leo
d. Capricorn

9 Which ancient civilization recorded the motion of the sun, moon, and planets on a wall in what is now **Guatemala?**

a. the Maya
b. the Egyptians
c. the Elnuit
d. the Chinese

10 In the Southern Hemisphere, you can spot a constellation in the shape of which **scientific** instrument?

a. microscope
b. telescope
c. compass
d. all of the above

11 Which of these songs helped runaway slaves find the **North Star?**

a. *Follow the Drinking Gourd*
b. *Twinkle, Twinkle, Little Star*
c. *Itsy-Bitsy Spider*
d. *Jingle Bell Rock*

12 What is the nickname of **Sirius,** the brightest star in the sky?

a. Super Star
b. the Bowling Ball
c. Max
d. the Dog Star

13 True or false? The constellations will never change their **shapes.**

14 True or false? Your Zodiac sign and horoscope readings are based on a **3,000**-year-old calendar.

15 Which constellation is the largest in the night **sky?**

a. Aquila, the eagle
b. Hydra, the serpent
c. Cancer, the crab
d. Boo-boo, the clown

Nature in the BIG CITY

1 Which animal can be seen roaming the streets of Mumbai, India?

a. cows   c. kangaroos
b. alligators   d. tigers

2 How have city songbirds adapted to hear one another over loud traffic noises?

a. only coming out at night
b. using packing peanuts as earplugs
c. singing higher-pitched songs
d. not singing at all

3 True or false?
Cockroaches have a backup brain in their rear ends.

4 Which city can coyotes call home?
a. Chicago, Illinois
b. Portland, Oregon
c. Seattle, Washington
d. all of the above

5 True or false?
Each year, more people visit the Grand Canyon in Arizona than the Eiffel Tower in Paris.

6 True or false?
Alligators thrive in the sewers below New York City.

7 Monkeys that live in cities in Zimbabwe often do what for fun?
a. play chess   c. play basketball
b. throw fruit   d. read books

8 In which urban location do peregrine falcons like to make their nests?
a. on the ground
b. in mailboxes
c. near Dumpsters
d. on top of high-rise buildings

CENTRAL PARK, NEW YORK CITY

9 Which European capital city boasts that it has the most trees?

a. London, England
b. Athens, Greece
c. Paris, France
d. Rome, Italy

10 Rats love cities! How many litters of pups can a healthy female rat produce every year?

a. 1   c. 50
b. 7   d. 100

11 True or false?
Clear glass windows cause more bird deaths than hunting house cats.

12 What can large amounts of pigeon droppings be used as?

a. fertilizer   c. glue
b. paint   d. confetti

13 True or false?
Trees can help keep city temperatures cooler in the summer.

14 Large colonies of which animal can often be found living under bridges in cities?

a. bats   c. armadillos
b. piranhas   d. penguins

15 Wild squirrels can't be found in which city?

a. São Paulo, Brazil
b. Hong Kong, China
c. Moscow, Russia
d. Sydney, Australia

CHECK YOUR ANSWERS ON PAGES 163–164.

MAP MANIA!

FAMOUS PARKS

U.S.

NORTH AMERICA

UNITED STATES

A

ATLANTIC OCEAN

PACIFIC OCEAN

SOUTH AMERICA

CHILE

B

1 SERENGETI NATIONAL PARK

Gazelles join which two animals on the Great Migration across the Serengeti plains every year?

a. turtles and alligators
b. lions and tigers
c. zebras and wildebeest
d. wild geese and turkeys

2 TORRES DEL PAINE NATIONAL PARK

Which animal is most closely related to the guanaco, which lives here?

a. camel
b. frog
c. goat
d. dog

3 KAKADU NATIONAL PARK

About how long have aboriginal people lived in the park, famous for its rock art?

a. 1,000 years
b. 5,000 years
c. 50,000 years
d. 100,000 years

ARCTIC OCEAN

SWITZERLAND

EUROPE
● C

A S I A

JAPAN
● E

PACIFIC OCEAN

AFRICA
● D
TANZANIA

INDIAN OCEAN

F ●
AUSTRALIA

④ FUJI-HAKONE-IZU NATIONAL PARK

More than 200,000 people climb to the top of Mount Fuji each year despite it being _____.

a. the steepest mountain in the world
b. an active volcano
c. closed to visitors
d. home to deadly poison dart frogs

⑤ GRAND CANYON NATIONAL PARK

What cut away this rock to form the deep gorge of the canyon?

a. dynamite
b. earthquakes
c. sandstorms
d. a flowing river

⑥ SWISS NATIONAL PARK

What are you not allowed to bring into the Swiss National Park?

a. a dog
b. a camera
c. bubble gum
d. a walking stick

7–12

MATCH EACH OF THESE ATTRACTIONS TO THE RED DOT THAT SHOWS ITS CORRECT LOCATION ON THE MAP.

TRUE or FALSE?

Into the Woods

1 BRISTLECONE PINE TREES CAN LIVE FOR MORE THAN 4,000 YEARS.

2 MORE THAN HALF OF THE PEOPLE WHO ATTEMPT TO HIKE THE ENTIRE APPALACHIAN TRAIL COMPLETE THE TRIP.

3 FOREST FIRES CAUSE JACK PINE TREES TO RELEASE THEIR SEEDS.

4 AN AREA OF WOODLANDS THE SIZE OF A CITY BLOCK MAY CONTAIN 60,000 SPIDERS.

5 HIBERNATING BLACK BEARS CAN GO FOR 6 MONTHS WITHOUT EATING.

6 THE FOREST-DWELLING BANANA SLUG OF THE NORTHERN PACIFIC COAST OF THE U.S.A. CAN GROW TO MORE THAN 20 INCHES (50.8 CM).

7 THE TALLEST REDWOOD TREE REACHES HIGHER THAN THE BIG BEN CLOCK TOWER IN LONDON, ENGLAND.

8 MANY TREE LEAVES CHANGE COLOR IN THE FALL TO HELP ATTRACT BIRDS AND INSECTS.

9 MORE THAN 10 PERCENT OF THE LAND ON EARTH IS COVERED WITH BOREAL FOREST, ALSO KNOWN AS THE TAIGA.

10 GREAT GRAY OWL CHICKS CLIMB OR FALL OUT OF THEIR NEST BEFORE THEY CAN FLY.

11 THE TRUNK OF GENERAL SHERMAN, A GIANT SEQUOIA TREE IN CALIFORNIA, U.S.A., WEIGHS AS MUCH AS 15 ADULT BLUE WHALES.

12 A FLYING SNAKE CAN GLIDE TWICE AS FAR AS A FLYING SQUIRREL.

13 CHICKEN-OF-THE-WOODS IS THE NAME OF A WILD GROUND BIRD.

14 ONE TREE PRODUCES ENOUGH OXYGEN IN AN HOUR FOR 100 PEOPLE TO BREATHE COMFORTABLY.

15 PEOPLE IN SUDAN USE MORINGA TREE SEEDS TO CLEAN WATER.

16 A PINE NEEDLE CAN CAPTURE MORE SUNLIGHT EACH DAY THAN AN OAK LEAF.

17 STICKY PINE SAP OFTEN TRAPS AND KILLS BEETLES THAT BURROW INTO A PINE TREE.

18 SOME TYPES OF SALAMANDERS CAN BREATHE THROUGH THEIR SKIN.

19 WHITE-TAILED DEER GET A RASH IF THEY TOUCH POISON IVY.

20 THE BLACK FOREST, OR SCHWARZWALD, IS IN GERMANY.

21 NATIVE AMERICANS TAUGHT COLONISTS HOW TO COLLECT SAP FROM SUGAR MAPLE TREES.

22 DENDROCHRONOLOGISTS ARE SCIENTISTS WHO STUDY ANIMAL TEETH.

23 ONE SPECIES OF CICADA ONLY EMERGES FROM THE GROUND EVERY 17 YEARS.

24 MOST DEER SPECIES GROW A NEW SET OF ANTLERS EVERY YEAR.

25 FIDDLEHEADS ARE NOISY FOREST INSECTS.

26 PETRIFIED WOOD, WHICH COMES FROM FOSSILIZED TREES, IS HARDER THAN DIAMONDS.

27 REDWOODS HAVE THE LARGEST LEAVES OF ANY TREE.

28 IN AUSTRALIA, SCIENTISTS DISCOVERED A TREE THAT HAS GOLD INSIDE ITS LEAVES.

29 IN 2013, SCIENTISTS DISCOVERED 8 NEW MAMMAL SPECIES IN THE CLOUD FORESTS OF PERU.

30 PLANTING A TREE IN YOUR YARD CAN HELP FIGHT GLOBAL WARMING.

CHECK YOUR ANSWERS ON PAGES 163–164.

GAME SHOW
ULTIMATE NATURE CHALLENGE

1 What is the British name for the group of stars also known as the **Big Dipper?**
a. the bathtub
b. the Plough
c. Dee Dee
d. the Queen

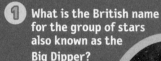

2 The wallaby is an animal native to which continent?
a. Australia
b. Antarctica
c. Europe
d. South America

3 Which U.S. state has the most national parks?
a. Utah
b. California
c. Hawaii
d. North Dakota

NATIONAL PARK SERVICE

Department of the Interior

4 One reason that zebras have black and white stripes is _____ .
a. to look prettier than horses
b. to keep insects away
c. to attract lions and tigers
d. all of the above

5 Old Faithful, an attraction at Yellowstone National Park, is a _____ .
a. geyser
b. tame black bear
c. gold mine
d. statue of Lassie the dog

6 Which animal does not live in or around the Great Barrier Reef?
a. sea turtle
b. shark
c. penguin
d. clownfish

7 The constellation Centaurus is named for a mythical creature that was _____ .
a. a pink horse with wings
b. a lion with a snake's head
c. a giant frog
d. half horse and half human

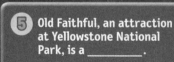

9 A hydrothermal vent is a crack in the seafloor that _____.
a. sucks in small fish
b. contains sharp spikes of rock
c. connects to another dimension
d. spews out hot water

8 TRUE OR FALSE?
It never snows in the Gobi in China and Mongolia.

11 On average, which force of nature kills the fewest people each year?
a. lightning strikes
b. extreme heat
c. severe cold
d. floods

10 Baobab trees of the African savanna can often survive _____.
a. tornadoes
b. droughts
c. earthquakes
d. swarms of locusts

12 What is one warning sign of an approaching tsunami?
a. the ocean becomes completely calm
b. birds stop singing
c. seawater gets sucked rapidly out into the ocean
d. a tornado forms over the ocean

13 Which animal do you regularly find in concrete jungles?
a. tiger   c. lion
b. human   d. rattlesnake

15 ULTIMATE BRAIN BUSTER
The pale white line in this rock circles Earth and marks what event that killed the dinosaurs?
a. an asteroid strike
b. the Ice Age
c. an attack of killer bees
d. a flood

14 TRUE OR FALSE?
Fluorescent fish create their own light in the deep ocean.

Back in TIME

PRESENTING A DRAFT OF THE
DECLARATION OF INDEPENDENCE
TO CONGRESS, JUNE 1776

Fashion FADS

1 What was the name of the haircut popular among males in the 1980s and 1990s that was short at the front and long at the back?

a. mully
b. mullo
c. mullet
d. moolah

2 In the early 1500s, women in Venice, Italy, wore thick-soled, extremely tall shoes. What did they bring with them to aid balance when walking?

a. a cane
b. an umbrella
c. a person to hold on to
d. a pair of socks

3 What odd fashion trend for young boys did the 1954 U.S. Western-themed TV show *Davy Crockett* inspire?

a. furry caps with raccoon tails
b. Native American–style face paint
c. bright red cowboy hats
d. cactus shoes

4 In the early 1980s, girls loved wearing these brightly colored "socks without feet" above their shoes. What were they called?

a. leg warmers
b. shin wrappers
c. feet shaders
d. knee fallers

5 **True or false?** In the 1600s, bald-headed French kings started wearing big powdered wigs.

6 **True or false?** In the 2000s, "Crocs" were popular fur-lined boots for women.

7 Which of these was a popular kind of bracelet in the 1990s?

a. built-in-video-game bracelet
b. slap bracelet that curled when slapped on the wrist
c. bracelet made out of colorful rubber bands
d. bracelet with photos on it

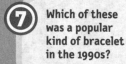

8 What was the hairstyle called that the queen of France, Marie Antoinette, wore in the late 1770s that was up to 4 feet (1.2 m) high?
a. hill
b. pouf
c. hairdon't
d. beehive

9 In the mid-1850s, women liked wearing skirts that reached down to the floor and were extremely wide. The bottom could be 6 feet (1.8 m) across! These skirts were known as crinoline _____.
a. megaphones
b. tents
c. cages
d. bells

10 **True or false?** In the 1960s, as NASA was gearing up to send astronauts to the moon, futuristic space clothes became popular.

11 In the 1920s, many young women cut their hair short and wore short skirts and lots of makeup. What was the name of this fashion group?
a. Gibson Girls
b. flappers
c. jazzers
d. clippers

12 Which of these was an actual mid-1980s fashion trend?
a. laceless shoes
b. fingerless gloves
c. pocketless pants
d. tie-dyed shirts

13 In the late 1960s and early 1970s, everybody wanted to wear bell-bottoms—pants that were very wide at the bottom. Who originally wore that style?
a. bell ringers in towers
b. dancers
c. sailors to take boots off quickly
d. people with very wide ankles

FAMOUS PETS

1 What powerful pet was kept by the **pharaoh** of Egypt, Ramesses II, in the 1200s B.C.?

a. hawk
b. lion
c. cobra
d. squirrel

2 A later pharaoh, Ptolemy II, paraded his pet through city streets. What colorful **creature** was it?

a. white bear
b. gray rhino
c. green parrot
d. blue whale

3 Nero, emperor of ancient Rome, had a **pet tiger**. What was its name?

a. Romeo
b. Stripey
c. Tigger
d. Phoebe

4 **True or false?** Joan of Arc, heroic leader of French troops in the early 1400s, was afraid of animals.

5 In the 1939 movie *The Wizard of Oz*, what did Dorothy's pet dog, **Toto**, jump out of to escape Miss Gulch?

a. a balloon
b. a first-story window
c. a basket on a bike
d. a slow train

6 In the popular *Scooby-Doo* cartoons, what is Scooby the dog's favorite **treat?**

a. chocolate chip cookies
b. Scooby Snacks
c. popcorn
d. lasagna

7 When composer Mozart's pet starling bird died in 1787, what did he do?

a. wrote a symphony based on its songs
b. purchased an identical bird
c. wrote a poem about it for the bird's funeral
d. got angry if anyone mentioned the bird

8 Joséphine Bonaparte, empress of France, had a pet orangutan! What was its favorite **food?**

a. bananas
b. turnips
c. strawberries
d. French fries

9 Who did Taylor Swift name her cat, Meredith, after?

a. her grandma
b. her best friend
c. a TV character
d. her math teacher

10 True or false? The first pet rabbit of Beatrix Potter, author of the Peter Rabbit stories, was named Benjamin Bouncer.

11 True or false? In 1968, Paul McCartney of the band the Beatles wrote a song about his pet **frog** named Michelle.

CHECK YOUR ANSWERS ON PAGES 164–165.

Toy STORY

KNUCKLEBONES, 300 B.C.

1 "Knucklebones" was a popular ancient game played with little pieces made of bone, glass, ivory, or other materials. How did kids play it?
- **a.** see how far you could toss the pieces
- **b.** find out how high you could stack them
- **c.** toss them in the air; see how many you could catch
- **d.** toss them in the air; see how many stayed in the air

2 A boomerang is a curved throwing stick that comes back to you. Where did it get its name?
- **a.** from a native tribe in Australia
- **b.** from its inventor, Hans Boomreng
- **c.** name of the tree the wood came from
- **d.** from the sound it makes hitting a bell

BOOMERANG

3 A popular board game from the ancient world, played with dice, is known as "Game of Twenty Squares." What was the goal of the game?
- **a.** get three squares in a row, like tic-tac-toe
- **b.** get to the other end of the board the fastest
- **c.** try to land in all the squares
- **d.** collect the most points as you move around the board

4 Some of the earliest dolls, from about 2000 B.C., were found in Egypt. Modern people call them "paddle dolls." Why?
- **a.** they were paddles used on Nile River boats
- **b.** the Egyptian word for the doll sounds like "paddle"
- **c.** they were flat and paddle-shaped
- **d.** children paddled with them in the bath

5 It is believed the first kites were made by a man named Lu Pan in China in about 400 B.C. What did he make them in the shape of?
- **a.** clouds
- **b.** birds
- **c.** faces
- **d.** string

KITES

6 For the holidays in 2009, the most popular toy was called Zhu Zhu. What was it?
- **a.** video game played with brainwaves
- **b.** robotic hamster
- **c.** 3-D hologram puzzle
- **d.** sneezing doll

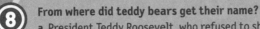

7 **True or false?** The game of marbles was invented by Sam Dyke in Akron, Ohio, U.S.A., in 1884.

8 **From where did teddy bears get their name?**
a. President Teddy Roosevelt, who refused to shoot a bear on a hunting trip
b. young Ted, son of the teddy bear store's owners
c. the name of the breed of small, gentle bears
d. Tedi, Austria, where the first one was made

TEDDY BEAR

9 **In 1956, Play-Doh was first introduced in Cincinnati, Ohio, U.S.A. But what was the original purpose of this substance?**
a. crack filler
b. chewing gum
c. wallpaper cleaner
d. bread dough

10 **In 1958, William Higinbotham invented *Tennis for Two*, possibly the world's first video game! Why did he invent it?**
a. to help students at his tennis camp
b. as his entry for a new-game contest
c. to entertain visitors to his science lab
d. to have fun at work

11 **Invented in 1959, where did the Barbie doll get its name?**
a. from Barbara, daughter of the doll's inventor, Ruth Handler
b. from James Barbie, designer of the doll
c. from barbecues, where the dolls were meant to be played with
d. from the barbells at the inventor's gym

12 **Ernö Rubik invented the Rubik's Cube in Budapest, Hungary, in 1974. What name did he give to the toy?**
a. Color Cube
b. Magic Cube
c. Rubik's Rectangle
d. Super Fun SlideBox

13 **True or false?** In 1996, Pokémon was introduced in Japan as a series of collectible trading cards.

BARBIE DOLL

BLAST FROM THE PAST
POMPEII

1 On August 24, in the year A.D. 79, a volcano erupted and buried the city of Pompeii in Italy. What was the name of the volcano?

a. Mount Everest
b. Mount St. Helens
c. Mount Vesuvius
d. Mount Rushmore

2 Residents tried to clear away the falling volcanic ash, but it was no use. At about what rate did ash fall on the city?

a. 1 inch (2.5 cm) an hour
b. 2 inches (5 cm) an hour
c. 6 inches (15 cm) an hour
d. 20 inches (50 cm) an hour

3 In what year did explorers rediscover Pompeii, perfectly preserved under layers of volcanic dust and ash?

a. 403   c. 1927
b. 1748   d. 2013

4 Located 5 miles (8 km) from the volcano, about 20,000 people lived in Pompeii. What sort of town was it?

a. a resort for important people from Rome
b. a key military base
c. Italy's main center of business
d. a suburb where local people lived

5 Pompeii was not the only city buried by the volcano! What was the name of the other ash-coated town?

a. Torre del Greco   c. Naples
b. Herculaneum   d. Rome

6 **True or false?** We know what happened when the volcano buried Pompeii from stories in a newspaper that was preserved by the ash.

7 What is especially famous about the walls in Pompeii?
a. they held back lava that would've destroyed the city
b. many were covered with ancient graffiti
c. they were not buried by ash
d. there were posted signs about what to do if the volcano erupted

8 True or false? In the 1700s, it was popular in England for families to build rooms in their homes similar to a style from Pompeii.

9 What was found in Pompeii that was very rare in the world at that time?
a. an early pipe system of "running water"
b. a zoo
c. a 10-story building
d. a primitive barber shop

10 Using plaster, archaeologists in 1874 made a model of _____ from Pompeii standing exactly as it was when the volcanic ash fell.
a. a horse
b. an elephant
c. a dog
d. a chicken

11 True or false? The volcano that buried Pompeii has erupted more than once. The most recent time was in 1881.

12 True or false? Archaeologists have found preserved loaves of bread and jars of fruit in Pompeii.

13 Many structures were uncovered in Pompeii. Which of the following Pompeii buildings collapsed in 2010?
a. House of the Surgeon
b. House of the Gladiators
c. House of the Silver Wedding
d. House of the Dancing Faun

14 After hundreds of years of digging, about how much of Pompeii is still buried?
a. one-tenth
b. one-fifth
c. one-third
d. one-half

CHECK YOUR ANSWERS ON PAGES 164–165.

93

Let the GAMES BEGIN

1. Skiing goes back thousands of years. Researchers recently found a 4,000-year-old painting of a skier ____.
   a. on a mountain in China
   b. in a cave in Alaska
   c. on an island in Norway
   d. in a temple in Greece

2. The first Olympic Games were held in Olympia, Greece, in 776 B.C. What was the one event held at those games?
   a. wrestling
   b. running
   c. long jump
   d. tennis

3. In China, from 220 B.C. to 206 B.C., "Tsu' Chu" was a popular game. What modern sport was it similar to?
   a. soccer (football)
   b. American football
   c. basketball
   d. water polo

ATHLETES ON AN ANCIENT GREEK POT

4. Mary, Queen of Scotland from 1542 to 1567, loved to play golf. What do many believe was her important contribution to the game?
   a. little dimples on the golf ball
   b. putting golf clubs in a bag
   c. calling the assistants who carried the clubs "caddies"
   d. digging little holes on the course

5. True or false? "Stoolball" is the name of an old English game that may have influenced baseball.

6. Hockey was named after an old French word for "stick." What important change happened to ice hockey in about 1860 in Canada?
   a. the stick was angled for the first time
   b. played with a puck instead of a ball
   c. played indoors for the first time
   d. players began wearing skates

7. In 1891, Dr. James Naismith invented the game of basketball in Springfield, Massachusetts, U.S.A. The baskets he used were peach baskets. What was the ball?
   a. a peach
   b. a crumpled newspaper
   c. a soccer ball
   d. a football

8 On September 6, 1995, baseball star Cal Ripken, Jr., broke a record that had existed since 1939. What was it?

a. most home runs in a season
b. getting a hit in the most games in a row without missing one
c. most errors in one inning
d. playing the most games in a row

9 **True or false?** College football leagues changed the rules in late 1905, making a touchdown worth 6 points.

10 At the 1976 Olympics, 14-year-old Romanian gymnast Nadia Comaneci became a superstar by winning the uneven-bar competition. What was so special about her performance?

a. first gold medal for Romania
b. youngest winner at the Olympics
c. first perfect score of "10"
d. she wore a blindfold

11 James Naismith had a friend in school named William Morgan. In 1895, what sport did Morgan invent?

a. volleyball   c. field hockey
b. karate   d. dodgeball

12 In 2002 and 2003, tennis superstar Serena Williams did the "Serena Slam." What was this?

a. not losing a single match
b. playing her sister Venus in ten championships
c. winning all four major tennis tournaments
d. going to NBA arenas and slam-dunking a basketball

13 **True or false?** Swimmer Michael Phelps broke the record for most Olympic medals when he won his 19th overall medal during the 2012 Summer Games.

MICHAEL PHELPS

CHECK YOUR ANSWERS ON PAGES 164–165.

Read All About It!

1. ONE OF THE EARLIEST KNOWN WORKS OF LITERATURE, *THE EPIC OF GILGAMESH*, FROM ABOUT 2000 B.C., TELLS OF A MAN SEARCHING FOR ETERNAL LIFE.

2. IN *AESOP'S FABLES*, THE TALES OF A GREEK SLAVE BORN ABOUT 620 B.C., ONE STORY IS ABOUT A JEALOUS MONKEY THAT TURNED INTO A ROOSTER.

3. THE TALE OF ALADDIN AND HIS MAGIC LAMP GOES BACK TO STORIES CALLED *ONE THOUSAND AND ONE NIGHTS* FROM THE 9TH CENTURY.

4. THE VIKINGS WROTE DOWN THEIR HEROIC TALES IN "THE SAGAS" IN NORWAY ABOUT THE YEAR A.D. 900.

5. IN THE BOOK *DON QUIXOTE* BY MIGUEL DE CERVANTES OF SPAIN, THE HERO DON QUIXOTE ATTACKS SOME WINDMILLS THAT HE THINKS ARE GIANTS.

6. ALL OF THE PLANETS IN OUR SOLAR SYSTEM ARE NAMED AFTER GREEK OR ROMAN GODS.

7. IN THE POPULAR 1977 BOOK *BRIDGE TO TERABITHIA* BY KATHERINE PATERSON, ONE CHARACTER GIVES ANOTHER THE CHRONICLES OF NARNIA STORIES TO READ.

8. IN NORSE MYTHOLOGY (OF THE SCANDINAVIAN PEOPLE), THOR IS CONSIDERED THE KING OF THE GODS.

9. A PRINTING PRESS INVENTED IN 1448 BY A GERMAN, JOHANNES GUTENBERG, MADE IT POSSIBLE TO PRODUCE BOOKS QUICKLY AND CHEAPLY FOR THE FIRST TIME.

10. IN THE DAYS OF PLAYWRIGHT WILLIAM SHAKESPEARE (1564–1616), ALL STAGE ROLES WERE PLAYED BY MEN—EVEN THE FEMALE CHARACTERS.

11. THERE HAVE BEEN THREE DIFFERENT MOVIE VERSIONS OF ROALD DAHL'S CLASSIC 1964 BOOK, *CHARLIE AND THE CHOCOLATE FACTORY*.

12. DANIEL DEFOE'S ADVENTURE STORY *ROBINSON CRUSOE*, FROM 1719, WAS THE FIRST BOOK WRITTEN IN ENGLISH.

13. IN *GULLIVER'S TRAVELS*, WRITTEN BY JONATHAN SWIFT IN 1726, THE LILLIPUTIAN PEOPLE ARE 12 INCHES (30 CM) TALL.

14. IN *CHARLOTTE'S WEB* BY E.B. WHITE FROM 1952, CHARLOTTE THE SPIDER WRITES "SOME PIG" IN HER WEB.

15. BRITISH AUTHOR MARY SHELLEY'S FAMOUS BOOK, PUBLISHED IN 1818, WAS ABOUT A MONSTER NAMED FRANKENSTEIN.

16 THE WORLD'S FIRST COMIC BOOK WAS *THE ADVENTURES OF MR. OBADIAH OLDBUCK*, PUBLISHED IN 1842.

17 THE ADVENTURE BOOKS *THE COUNT OF MONTE CRISTO* AND *THE THREE MUSKETEERS* WERE BOTH WRITTEN BY FRANCE'S ALEXANDRE DUMAS, IN 1844.

18 WE ALMOST NEVER GOT TO READ ROBERT LOUIS STEVENSON'S *DR. JEKYLL AND MR. HYDE* BECAUSE HIS WIFE THREW THE FIRST VERSION INTO A FIRE.

19 LAURA INGALLS WILDER'S NINE-BOOK LITTLE HOUSE SERIES, PUBLISHED FROM 1932 TO 1943, WAS TURNED INTO A POPULAR TV SERIES IN THE 1970S.

20 BETWEEN WRITING *THE HOBBIT* (1937) AND *THE LORD OF THE RINGS* (1954), J.R.R. TOLKIEN WROTE A BROADWAY PLAY ABOUT A SINGING MULE.

21 ANTOINE DE SAINT-EXUPÉRY, THE FRENCH AUTHOR OF THE POPULAR CHILDREN'S STORY *THE LITTLE PRINCE* (1943), WAS ALSO A FAMOUS PILOT.

22 THE C.S. IN C.S. LEWIS—AUTHOR OF THE SEVEN CHRONICLES OF NARNIA BOOKS (1950–56)—STANDS FOR "CASPIAN STEVEN."

23 THE FIRST LIBRARY OF E-BOOKS BEGAN IN 1971, IN A COLLECTION CALLED "PROJECT GUTENBERG."

24 THE *MARY POPPINS* BOOK BY P. L. TRAVERS AND THE *MARY POPPINS* DISNEY MOVIE BOTH CAME OUT IN 1964.

25 J.K. ROWLING'S SEVEN-BOOK HARRY POTTER SERIES, PUBLISHED IN THE U.S.A. BETWEEN 1998 AND 2007, HAD A TOTAL OF 4,224 PAGES.

26 *PAGETURNER*, THE FIRST 24-HOUR TV NETWORK ABOUT BOOKS, WENT ON THE AIR IN 2003.

27 THE MORRIGAN IS THE GODDESS OF WAR IN IRISH MYTHOLOGY WHO CAN CHANGE INTO A CROW, EEL, OR COW.

28 IN THE MYTHOLOGY OF SWITZERLAND, THERE IS A CREATURE KNOWN AS TATZELWURM, WHO IS A WORM WITH CLAWS.

29 STEPHENIE MEYER NAMED THE FIRST BOOK IN HER FOUR-VOLUME SERIES *TWILIGHT* BECAUSE EVERY DAY SHE'D SIT DOWN TO WRITE AT TWILIGHT.

30 THE WORLD RECORD FOR THE LARGEST BOOK HAS IT AT 16.4 FEET BY 26.44 FEET (5 M BY 8 M), WEIGHING ABOUT 3,300 POUNDS (1,500 KG), AND WITH 429 PAGES.

CHECK YOUR ANSWERS ON PAGES 164–165.

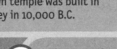

Lost WORLDS

SUMERIAN WRITING TABLET

1 **True or false?** The world's first known temple was built in Turkey in 10,000 B.C.

2 The Sumerian people of Mesopotamia (modern Iraq) are believed to have invented the earliest form of writing, using pictures. About when was this writing developed?

a. 5000 B.C.   c. 2000 B.C.
b. 3500 B.C.   d. A.D. 1200

MAYA CALENDAR

3 The Maya people, who lived in Central America from about 1000 B.C. to A.D. 900, developed a complex calendar. According to modern experts, on what day did the Maya calendar begin?

a. January 1, 1000 B.C.
b. December 21, 2012
c. August 11, 3114 B.C.
d. January 1 of the year 1

4 Which historical person some 2,300 years ago is believed to have totally made up the lost underwater world of Atlantis?

a. Greek philosopher Plato
b. Chinese philosopher Confucius
c. Greek philosopher Aristotle
d. Roman general Julius Caesar

5 Qin Shi Huangdi, China's first emperor (from 221 B.C. to 210 B.C.), had a giant underground city constructed, where he would be buried. With what did he choose to guard this secret tomb?

a. trained wolves   c. life-size clay soldiers
b. poisonous snakes   d. a "keep out" sign

6 **True or false?** More than 200 large shapes in the ground in the Amazon region of South America were carved there by people hundreds of years ago.

7 Árpád, who lived from about 850 to 907, was a chieftain of Russia's Magyar tribe. What is the modern name of the Magyars' homeland?

a. Hungary   c. Belgium
b. Turkey   d. France

QIN SHI HUANGDI

8 In 982, the Viking Erik the Red sailed to this country and gave it a name. What country was it?

a. Iceland **c.** Australia
b. Greenland **d.** Canada

EASTER ISLAND STATUE

9 Between about 1250 and 1500, Easter Islanders in the South Pacific Ocean built giant statues to honor their people and watch over the island. What is their name for these statues?

a. *tuff* **c.** *moai*
b. *tiki* **d.** *rushmore*

10 Nahuatl, the language of the Aztec people, was the most widely spoken in Mexico in the 1350s. Which one of these English words did *not* come from Nahuatl?

a. coyote **c.** cobra
b. chili **d.** avocado

KNIGHT IN ARMOR

11 Brave knights of the 1400s are known for their suits of armor. About how much did a full suit of armor weigh?

a. 17 pounds (8 kg) **c.** 110 pounds (50 kg)
b. 50 pounds (23 kg) **d.** 300 pounds (136 kg)

12 True or false? Archaeologists believe that tree houses found deep in the Canadian forest were left behind by a secret group of settlers in the 1530s.

13 The Ashanti people of Ghana, Africa, have a sacred symbol that is said to have come down from heaven into the lap of the first Ashanti king. What is the sacred symbol?

a. a golden stool **c.** a cat
b. a dove **d.** a tree

CHECK YOUR ANSWERS ON PAGES 164–165.

PARTY TIME!

1 In China, during September's Mid-Autumn Festival, the traditional food served is _____.
a. little round "mooncakes"
b. roasted corn
c. orange-colored "ice treats"
d. mid-mints

2 Since the 1500s, what has been a big part of the Midsummer celebration held in late June in **Sweden**?
a. wearing animal masks
b. baking a summer pie
c. dancing around a decorated pole
d. playing a calendar darts game

3 True or false? During the month-long Magh Mela Festival in India, thousands of people bathe in the Ganges River.

4 During the Japanese girls' festival Hina-matsuri, traditionally what items were placed in a boat to send away bad spirits?
a. flowers
b. rocks
c. dolls
d. life preservers

CHINESE DRAGON LIGHTS

5 Krampus is an Austrian holiday character that dates back to the 1600s. Who is he?
a. Santa's friendly grandpa
b. the goat that leads Santa's sleigh
c. a creature who punishes naughty children
d. a funny witch

6 What is famously **decorated** for the Esala Perahera festival held in Sri Lanka since 1775?

a. trees
b. elephants
c. houses
d. spoons

7 On the last Tuesday of January in Lerwick, Scotland, the Up Helly Aa **festival** highlights _____.

a. an apple-pie-eating contest
b. the burning of a Viking ship
c. racing up a small mountain
d. a snowball fight

8 Masked dancers are part of the Indra Jatra festival in **Nepal** that celebrates the _____.

a. end of the rainy season
b. birthday of musician Indra Jatra
c. tribute to music and dance
d. invention of the mask

9 True or false? At an annual festival in Binche, Belgium, people throw strawberries at men wearing **wax masks.**

10 What has been a New Year's Eve tradition in Germany since 1972?

a. walking across a bridge at midnight
b. watching a 1963 British comedy show on TV
c. singing that year's No. 1 song at 12:15 a.m.
d. saying "Happy 1973!"

11 True or false? In the Netherlands in 2014, Koninginnedag (Queen's Day) was changed to Koningsdag (King's Day) because the country now has a male ruler.

CHECK YOUR ANSWERS ON PAGES 164–165.

MAP MANIA!
ROTTEN RULERS

History is filled with leaders who were not good to their people. See if you can answer these questions about rotten rulers from around the world.

① RAMESSES II
1303 B.C.–1213 B.C.

This pharaoh is most remembered for his

_____.

a. use of slaves
b. human sacrifices
c. poisoning of his father
d. all of the above

NORTH AMERICA

A ●

ATLANTIC OCEAN

SOUTH AMERICA

PACIFIC OCEAN

② MOCTEZUMA
C. 1466–1520

What finally stopped this cruel emperor of the Aztecs?

a. a mysterious illness
b. defeat by the Spanish explorer Hernán Cortés
c. falling off his horse Tenochtitlan and being badly injured
d. losing the Aztec election of 1520

③ IVAN THE TERRIBLE
1530–1584

The rage-filled first tsar (leader) of Russia grabbed land through violence and terror. What was his nickname?

a. Grozny   c. Musco
b. Terry   d. Tsar-Tsar Binks

4 GHENGIS KHAN
C. 1162–1227

The fierce army leader and builder of the Mongol Empire had many, many children. How many men in modern times are related to Genghis Khan?

a. 1 out of every 1 million
b. 1 out of every 500,000
c. 1 out of every 200
d. 1

ARCTIC OCEAN

EUROPE

C

E

A

S

I

F

D

AFRICA

B

PACIFIC OCEAN

INDIAN OCEAN

AUSTRALIA

5 VLAD THE IMPALER
1431–1476

Vlad killed his enemies using a long wooden pole. What fictional character was Vlad the inspiration for?

a. Darth Vader
b. Dracula
c. Dr. Frankenstein
d. Cobra Commander

6 IDI AMIN
C. 1925–2003

On joining the army and before becoming a ruthless president of Uganda in 1971, what was Amin's job?

a. guard at the front gate
b. radio specialist
c. assistant cook
d. clothes washer

7–12 MATCH THESE ROTTEN RULERS FROM HISTORY TO THE DOT THAT SHOWS HIS COUNTRY OR AREA OF RULE ON THE MAP.

GAME SHOW

ULTIMATE TIME TRAVEL CHALLENGE

1 What was the name for this style of shoes from the late 1960s and early 1970s?
a. hello-down-theres
b. platforms
c. elevators
d. boosters

2 Which U.S. president kept a little zoo at the White House featuring a one-legged rooster?
a. Abraham Lincoln
b. Franklin Roosevelt
c. Teddy Roosevelt
d. George W. Bush

3 Seventeen years before the volcano eruption buried Pompeii, what other natural disaster had hit the city?
a. earthquake
b. hurricane
c. tornado
d. wildfire

4 In which country did this toy get its common name?
a. the U.S.A.
b. the Philippines
c. Mexico
d. Mozambique

5 TRUE OR FALSE?

Before the lawnmower was invented in 1830, grass sports fields were often kept short using this pictured animal.

6 Which of these stories was *not* in the *Tales of My Mother Goose* written in 1697 by Charles Perrault of France?
a. Little Red Riding Hood
b. Peter Pan
c. Sleeping Beauty
d. Cinderella

7 According to legend, in which country is the lost gold ransom for the Inca king Atahualpa of the 1500s?
a. Ecuador
b. Colombia
c. Venezuela
d. Uruguay

9 TRUE OR FALSE?

In Italy in the 1910s, it was fashionable to wear socks over your shoes.

8 In China, what decoration is on the front of boats raced in a festival dating back to 278 B.C.?

a. an open book
b. a glowing star
c. a dragon's head
d. a giant donut

10 Lassie the collie dog, from a short story of 1938, has *not* starred in_____.

a. a TV series
b. a movie
c. a Broadway musical
d. a radio show

11 Which of these items was inducted into the U.S.A.'s National Toy Hall of Fame in 2013?

a. Magic 8 Ball
b. rubber duck
c. Pac-Man video game
d. My Little Pony

13 TRUE OR FALSE?

The stories "The Legend of Sleepy Hollow" and "Rip Van Winkle" were written by the same person.

12 When did Mount Vesuvius erupt before erupting in A.D. 79 and burying the city of Pompeii?

a. A.D. 23
b. 208 B.C.
c. 1780 B.C.
d. 12,000 B.C.

15 ULTIMATE BRAIN BUSTER

For the Tamborrada festival in San Sebastián, Spain, which of these do many drummers wear?

a. fireman's hat

c. cowboy hat

b. chef's hat

d. flowery hat

14 From 690 to 705, China had a leader who is rumored to have been very cruel. But what is this leader most remembered for?

a. ordered construction of the Great Wall of China
b. was the only female leader in China's history: Empress Wu
c. walked to Japan to get back stolen riches
d. invented a dance later known as "The Twist"

We've Got Your NUMBER

107

Color by NUMBERS

1. How many gallons (or liters) of white paint does it take to cover the outside of the White House?
   a. 24 gallons (91 L)
   b. 570 gallons (2,158 L)
   c. 1,600 gallons (6,056 L)
   d. that is classified information

BLUE LOBSTER

2. A man in England filmed children, a bird, and a fish as the first movie ever in color! What year was this?
   a. 1624
   b. 1902
   c. 1960
   d. 1982

3. Of all the lobsters in the world, how many are born blue?
   a. one in every thousand
   b. one in every million
   c. one in every 2 million
   d. one in every 16 billion

4. What percent of the land in Greenland is covered with ice?
   a. 10 percent
   b. 50 percent
   c. 80 percent
   d. 100 percent

GREENLAND

5. True or false?
   About 1 in every 100 people worldwide has red hair.

6. In 2013, the world's largest orange-colored diamond was sold for $35.5 million. It's about the size of _____.
   a. a coconut
   b. a shoebox
   c. an almond
   d. an orange

TOY NEW YORK TAXI

7 How many official yellow taxis are there in New York City?
a. 13,237
b. 603
c. 5,024
d. one really, really busy taxi

8 How many tie-dyed T-shirts can be made from a bale of cotton, which weighs about 500 pounds (227 kg)?
a. 12
b. 121
c. 1,217
d. 12,170

9 What distance is the new event "The Color Run," in which runners are showered with colored powder?
a. 109 yards (100 m)
b. 3.2 miles (5.1 km)
c. 26.2 miles (42.2 km)
d. one step

10 True or false?
A brown bear can run 35 miles an hour (55 km/h).

11 True or false?
Dogs can see only one color: gray.

BROWN BEAR

12 In 2003, the world's largest crayon was unveiled at Crayola headquarters in Pennsylvania, U.S.A. How tall was it?
a. 15 feet (4.6 m)
b. 6 feet (1.8 m)
c. 64 feet (19.5 m)
d. 301 feet (91.7 m)

13 In what year was the first national color television broadcast in the U.S.A.?
a. 1927
b. 1954
c. 1964
d. 1776

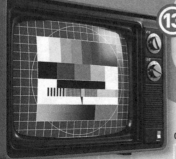

COLOR TELEVISION

CHECK YOUR ANSWERS ON PAGES 166–167.

Mount Rushmore MATH

1 About how many workers helped sculptor Gutzon Borglum make the national memorial in the Black Hills of South Dakota, U.S.A.?

a. 5
b. 28
c. 400
d. he worked alone

2 In the original plan, how many U.S. presidents were to be represented on Mount Rushmore?

a. 1 (Washington)
b. 2 (Washington and Lincoln)
c. 4 (they followed the original plan)
d. 30 (all of them up to the date they started building)

3 Work on Mount Rushmore began on October 4, 1927. How long did it take to complete?

a. they are still working on it
b. 17 months
c. 14 years
d. one week

4 How much of Mount Rushmore was carved using dynamite?

a. 5 percent
b. 25 percent
c. 90 percent
d. 110 percent

5 The monument was named after a New York lawyer, Charles E. Rushmore, in _____ ?

a. 1885
b. 1492
c. 1927
d. 2008

6 What was the total cost of making Mount Rushmore?

a. $25,965.34
b. $989,992.32
c. $14,319.78
d. $12

7 True or false?
If the presidential heads on Mount Rushmore were real people with bodies, they'd be 465 feet (141.7 m) tall.

8 In 1959 director Alfred Hitchcock built a model of Mount Rushmore on a Hollywood film set. About how much did the model cost?

a. $25,000   **c.** $15,000
b. $1,000,000   **d.** $12

9 How tall is Mount Rushmore from the ground to the top of the presidents' heads?

a. 815 feet (248.4 m)
b. 5,725 feet (1,745 m)
c. 12,208 feet (3,721 m)
d. it's never been measured

10 True or false?

The nearby giant sculpture of Lakota Indian Chief Crazy Horse was also designed by Gutzon Borglum.

11 To make the presidents' eyes twinkle, shafts were dug into the pupil of each eye to reflect sunlight. How deep are the eye shafts?

a. 2 inches (5 cm)   **c.** 2 yards (1.8 m)
b. 2 feet (61 cm)   **d.** 2 miles (3.2 km)

12 There were no goats around Mount Rushmore until some escaped from a nearby state park in 1924! About how many goats are in the area today?

a. 6   **c.** 200
b. 12   **d.** 25,000

13 What is the distance from Washington's right ear to Lincoln's left?

a. 6 feet (1.8 m)
b. 185 feet (56.4 m)
c. 400 feet (122 m)
d. we asked; they didn't hear

14 George Washington was about 6 feet (1.8 m) tall. How many times taller is his head on Mount Rushmore?

a. 1,000   **c.** 10
b. 100   **d.** it's shorter

15 In 1998, a "time capsule" about Mount Rushmore's history was placed behind the heads with a large stone on top. How heavy is the stone?

a. 200 pounds (90.7 kg)
b. 1,200 pounds (544.3 kg)
c. 5,000 pounds (2,268 kg)
d. 18 ounces (510.3 g)

WHAT'S COOKING?

1 The world's largest cheesecake was 7.5 feet (2.3 m) across and 31 inches (78.7 cm) deep. What was its **weight?**

a. 20 pounds (9.1 kg)
b. 6,900 pounds (3,129.8 kg)
c. 40,000 pounds (18,143.7 kg)
d. eaten before it was weighed

2 In what decade did Ruth Wakefield of the U.S.A. invent the chocolate-chip cookie?

a. 1930s   c. 1730s
b. 1830s   d. 30 B.C.

3 About what percent of the world's instant noodles are eaten in **China?**

a. 43 percent   c. 76 percent
b. 20 percent   d. 99 percent

4 How much milk does it take to make one gallon (3.8 L) of **ice cream?**

a. 1 cup (237 mL)   c. 12 pounds (5.4 kg)
b. 24 ounces (0.7 kg)   d. 1 gallon (3.8 L)

5 How much macaroni was used to make the **world's** largest macaroni and cheese?

a. 2,400 pounds (1,088.6 kg)
b. 575 pounds (260.8 kg)
c. 103 pounds (46.7 kg)
d. 16 ounces (453.6 g)

6 True or false?

The burrito was probably first made in Mexico and got its name in the late 1800s.

7 True or false? The average chicken lays about **700** eggs a year.

8 About how many peanuts does it take to make one 12-ounce (340-g) jar of **peanut butter?**

a. 40
b. 540
c. 5,040
d. 5,000,040

9 Mike Cuzzacrea of the U.S.A., known as the "Pancake Man," has tossed a pancake to a record height of _____ .

a. 22 feet (6.7 m)
b. 31 feet, 1 inch (9.5 mm)
c. 78 feet (23.8 mm)
d. 400 feet (122 m)

10 What temperature is milk when it comes out of a cow?

a. 97°F (36.1°C)
b. 212°F (100°C)
c. 31°F (−0.54°C)
d. 451°F (232.8°C)

11 The world's largest deliverable **pizza** is a square pie 54 inches (137.2 cm) per side. How many normal-size slices are in the pizza?

a. 50
b. 1,000
c. 200
d. 8

12 How many **bananas** were used in the world's largest smoothie?

a. 32
b. 3,200
c. 320,000
d. It was a strawberry smoothie. There were no bananas.

13 How much meat was used to make the world's largest meatball?

a. 1,110.5 pounds (503.7 kg)
b. 2,221 pounds (1,007.4 kg)
c. 1,492 pounds (676.8 kg)
d. 500 pounds (226.8 kg)

CHECK YOUR ANSWERS ON PAGES 166–167.

It's About Time

1 WORLD WAR II BEGAN WHEN GERMANY INVADED POLAND ON SEPTEMBER 1, 1939.

2 THE WORLD'S FASTEST LAND ANIMAL, THE CHEETAH, CAN RUN UP TO 100 MILES AN HOUR (161 KM/H).

3 PEOPLE AROUND THE WORLD WERE AFRAID THAT MANY COMPUTERS WOULD STOP AT MIDNIGHT ON DECEMBER 31, 1999.

4 OLD PENNIES ARE USED TO KEEP THE FAMOUS "BIG BEN" CLOCK IN LONDON AS ACCURATE AS POSSIBLE.

5 ON JULY 16, 1970, AT 10:56 P.M. EASTERN TIME, NEIL ARMSTRONG TOOK THE FIRST HUMAN STEP ON THE MOON.

6 WHILE DIVING, THE PEREGRINE FALCON IS THE FASTEST ANIMAL IN THE AIR, REACHING 270 MILES AN HOUR (434.5 KM/H).

7 ON OCTOBER 12, 1492, CHRISTOPHER COLUMBUS SET FOOT ON LAND THAT WOULD EVENTUALLY BE THE UNITED STATES OF AMERICA.

8 WORLD WAR I FORMALLY ENDED IN 1918, AT THE 11TH HOUR OF THE 11TH DAY OF THE 11TH MONTH: NOVEMBER 11, 11:00 A.M.

9 ABOUT EVERY YEAR AND A HALF, ONE SECOND—CALLED A LEAP SECOND—IS ADDED TO THE WORLD'S TIME TO KEEP IT ACCURATE.

10 THE MARLIN, WHICH CAN SWIM ABOUT 50 MILES AN HOUR (80.5 KM/H), IS THE WORLD'S FASTEST FISH.

11 THE UNITED STATES DECLARATION OF INDEPENDENCE WAS SIGNED ON JULY 4, 1776.

12 ON MIDNIGHT AS IT BECAME JULY 1 IN 1997, THE CITY OF HONG KONG RETURNED TO CHINESE CONTROL AFTER MORE THAN 150 YEARS OF BRITISH RULE.

13 ON AUGUST 13, 1961, THE BERLIN WALL THAT SEPARATED WEST GERMANY AND EAST GERMANY WAS FINALLY TORN DOWN.

14 ON MAY 6, 1954, ROGER BANNISTER OF BRITAIN BECAME THE FIRST PERSON TO RUN A MILE (1.6 KM) IN LESS THAN 3 MINUTES.

15 IN 1929, THE SOVIET UNION (WHICH IS NOW RUSSIA AND PARTS OF EASTERN EUROPE) BRIEFLY CHANGED THEIR CALENDAR TO FIVE-DAY WEEKS AND SIX-WEEK MONTHS.

16 THE FAMOUS SHIP R.M.S. *TITANIC* SUNK ON APRIL 10, 1912, JUST OVER TWO AND A HALF HOURS AFTER STRIKING AN ICEBERG.

17 IN BRITAIN, A PERIOD OF TWO WEEKS IS SOMETIMES CALLED A HALFUARY.

18 THE FIRST TELEPHONE CALL—BETWEEN INVENTOR ALEXANDER GRAHAM BELL AND HIS ASSISTANT, THOMAS WATSON—HAPPENED ON MARCH 10, 1901.

19 THE FASTEST TIME TO SOLVE A RUBIK'S CUBE—THE POPULAR TOY WHERE YOU NEED TO MAKE EACH SIDE OF THE CUBE A SINGLE COLOR—IS 5.5 SECONDS.

20 A HOPPING RED KANGAROO, WHICH CAN REACH 35 MILES AN HOUR (56.3 KM/H), IS FASTER THAN THE FASTEST HUMAN RUNNER.

21 EACH NEW DAY OFFICIALLY BEGINS ON CAROLINE ISLAND IN THE PACIFIC OCEAN, WHICH IS THE EASTERNMOST POINT ON LAND.

22 SU SONG OF CHINA BUILT THE WORLD'S FIRST CLOCK IN 1088.

23 WHILE HUMAN MOTHERS ARE PREGNANT FOR ABOUT 9 MONTHS, FRILLED SHARKS ARE BELIEVED TO BE PREGNANT FOR ABOUT 3.5 YEARS.

24 WATCHING HOW FAST DROPS OF TAR FALL IS THE WORLD'S LONGEST RUNNING LAB EXPERIMENT. IT HAS BEEN GOING ON IN AUSTRALIA SINCE 1927.

25 JACK SCHOFF OF THE U.S.A. OWNS THE WORLD'S LARGEST COLLECTION OF CLOCKS, WITH MORE THAN 1,500 IN HIS HOME.

26 THE WORD "MINUTE" COMES FROM HENRI MINET, A FRENCH TIMEKEEPER IN THE MID-1300S.

27 ON OCTOBER 14, 1947, U.S. AIR FORCE PILOT CHUCK YEAGER BECAME THE FIRST PERSON IN A PLANE TO GO FASTER THAN THE SPEED OF LIGHT.

28 THE COUNTRY OF NEPAL HAS ITS OWN TIME ZONE, THE ONLY ONE IN THE WORLD WITH A TIME 15 MINUTES DIFFERENT THAN IN A BORDERING COUNTRY.

29 NORTH KOREA USES A 13-MONTH CALENDAR.

30 A ROCKET MUST TRAVEL AT MORE THAN 25,000 MILES AN HOUR (40,233.6 KM/H) TO ESCAPE THE PULL OF EARTH'S GRAVITY.

CHECK YOUR ANSWERS ON PAGES 166–167.

Money MATTERS

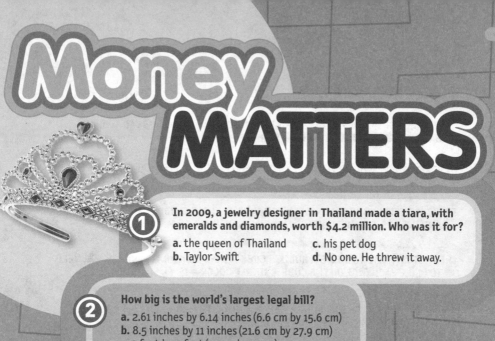

1 In 2009, a jewelry designer in Thailand made a tiara, with emeralds and diamonds, worth $4.2 million. Who was it for?

a. the queen of Thailand
b. Taylor Swift
c. his pet dog
d. No one. He threw it away.

2 How big is the world's largest legal bill?

a. 2.61 inches by 6.14 inches (6.6 cm by 15.6 cm)
b. 8.5 inches by 11 inches (21.6 cm by 27.9 cm)
c. 3 feet by 5 feet (0.9 m by 1.5 m)
d. 1 mile by 2 miles (1.6 km by 3.2 km)

3 In Freetown, Sierra Leone, most people trade with _____, not money.

a. wheat
b. cloth
c. water
d. wood

4 What do coin collectors call a "FIDO"?

a. the collector's dog
b. an error coin
c. the collector's assistant
d. dough used to make $5 worth of bread

5 What is the word for studying and collecting coins?

a. coinology
b. financiary
c. numismatics
d. heads-or-tailism

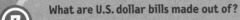

6 **True or false?**
Calling a U.S. dollar a "buck" comes from the time when Western traders used deerskins, called bucks, as currency.

7 **What are U.S. dollar bills made out of?**
a. wood pulp
b. 75 percent cotton/25 percent linen
c. artificial fibers
d. dirt

8 **True or false?**
Canadians call their $1 coin a "loonie."

CANADIAN DOLLAR

9 The world's most expensive sneakers, dipped in 18-carat gold, cost _____ .
a. $157   c. $100,017
b. $4,053   d. $1,000,000

10 **Before coins became popular, which of these items was used as money somewhere in the world?**
a. shells   c. tools
b. cattle   d. all of the above

11 In 2013, the family of Carlos Slim Helú of Mexico was worth $73 billion. In what business did it make most of its money?
a. restaurants   c. airlines
b. cell phones/Internet d. lemonade stand

12 **True or false?**
If you had a stack of 1 trillion U.S. dollar bills, it could wrap around Earth one time.

MAP MANIA!
SUPERSIZED STRUCTURES

Test your knowledge of scale with these supersized structures.

1 INDIANAPOLIS MOTOR SPEEDWAY

This is the largest sports facility in the world, with _____ seats.

a. 3,500
b. 235,000
c. 2,350,000
d. 35,000

NORTH AMERICA

SOUTH AMERICA

PACIFIC OCEAN

ATLANTIC OCEAN

D ● ● E

C ●

2 ONE WORLD TRADE CENTER

At 1,776 feet (541.3 m), how much taller is this building than Chicago's Willis Tower, previously the tallest in the U.S.A.?

a. 1,451 feet (442.3 m)
b. 1 foot (0.3 m)
c. 325 feet (99.1 m)
d. 2,000 feet (609.6 m)

3 MILLAU VIADUCT

This is the world's tallest bridge. What is the distance from the bottom of the valley to the top of the bridge?

a. 1,125 feet (342.9 m)
b. 1,125 inches (28.6 m)
c. 1,125 miles (1,810.5 km)
d. can't measure; we're afraid to look down.

④ AZTEC STADIUM

This soccer stadium, host to the World Cup final in 1970 and 1986, has a capacity of _____ .

a. 65,000   c. 105,000
b. 85,000   d. 125,000

ARCTIC OCEAN

EUROPE

B

ASIA

A

AFRICA

F

PACIFIC OCEAN

INDIAN OCEAN

AUSTRALIA

ANTARCTICA

⑥ BURJ KHALIFA

At 2,717 feet (828.1 m), this is the world's tallest building. How fast do its elevators travel?

a. 4 miles an hour (6.4 km/h)
b. 26.1 miles an hour (42.3 km/h)
c. 100 miles an hour (160.9 km/h)
d. Whoops, the elevator is stuck!

⑤ THREE GORGES DAM

To build the world's largest dam involved the removal of _____ .

a. 13 cities
b. 140 towns
c. 1,350 villages
d. all of the above

7–12 MATCH EACH OF THESE SUPERSIZED STRUCTURES TO THE RED DOT THAT SHOWS ITS CORRECT LOCATION ON THE MAP.

CHECK YOUR ANSWERS ON PAGES 166–167.

GAME SHOW
ULTIMATE GIANT CHALLENGE

1 Computer screens can display about 16.8 million different colors. But about how many different colors can the human eye actually see?
a. 18 million   c. 64
b. 10 million   d. 5

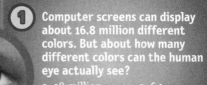

2 The heads on Mount Rushmore are 60 feet (18.3 m) tall. About how wide is each mouth?
a. 60 feet (18.3 m)
b. 3 inches (7.6 cm)
c. 18 feet (5.5 m)
d. 1 mile (1.6 km)

3 How much raw dough was used to make the world's largest pretzel, which was 26 feet, 10 inches (8.2 m) across?
a. 1.184 pounds (0.54 kg)
b. 11.84 pounds (5.4 kg)
c. 1,184 pounds (537.1 kg)
d. 118,400 pounds (53,705 kg)

4 A trip between two Japanese cities on this high-speed train now takes 95 minutes. On a faster version, ready in 2027, how long will the same trip take?
a. 40 minutes   b. 1 minute
                   c. 2 hours
                   d. 2 seconds

5 How often is a "blue moon"?
a. once a month
b. once a year
c. on the second full moon in a month
d. once every 10 years

7 In 2013, a collector paid $52 million for a 1960s Ferrari 250 GTO. About how many new Ferraris could you buy with $52 million?
a. sorry, the same collector just bought them all
b. 5,000
c. 176
d. 2

6 TRUE OR FALSE?
From 1899 to 1974, the world's tallest building was located in New York City, U.S.A.

120

8 After 18 months of carving Thomas Jefferson's head on Mount Rushmore, what happened?

a. Jefferson's "smile" was toned down
b. workers dynamited it and started again
c. Jefferson's descendants visited the site
d. the nose fell off

9 In cooking, how many teaspoons equal a tablespoon?
a. 4   b. 3   c. 2   d. 1

10 # TRUE OR FALSE?
U.S. coins are made from metals but a "nickel" has no nickel in it.

11 # TRUE OR FALSE?
The faces on Mount Rushmore represent the U.S.A.'s first four presidents.

12 At 15.23 miles (24.5 km), Laerdal Tunnel is the world's longest tunnel that you can drive through. Where is it?

a. in the U.S.A.
b. in Switzerland
c. in Norway
d. it starts in Germany and ends in Belgium

13 What is the greatest number of Friday the 13ths that can occur in a single year?

a. 3
b. 2
c. 4
d. none, if you're lucky!

14 On April 12, 1961, Yuri Gagarin of Russia made the first spaceflight. How long was the flight?

a. 10 minutes
b. 108 minutes
c. 3 hours, 20 minutes
d. he is still traveling in space

15 ULTIMATE BRAIN BUSTER
Which of these is the most popular car color in North America.

a.   b.   c.   d.

TRICERATOPS GRAZING

Amazing SCIENCE

I HEARD ON THE NEWS THAT THERE MAY BE AN ASTEROID COMING. IT MIGHT CHANGE A FEW THINGS!

DINOSAUR DAYS

1 What did the armored dinosaur *Ankylosaurus* likely use its clubbed tail to do?
a. climb trees
b. fight off predators
c. catch fish
d. dig holes

2 On which modern continent did *Protoceratops* roam?
a. Australia
b. Antarctica
c. Asia
d. the moon

3 True or false?
When dinosaurs ruled the world, there were no birds flying around.

4 True or false?
A great white shark has a stronger bite than a *Tyrannosaurus rex* had.

5 *Megalodon* was a giant prehistoric relative of a _____.
a. shark   c. cow
b. gorilla   d. penguin

6 What is the largest number of quarter-pound hamburger patties that a *Tyrannosaurus rex* could gobble up in a single bite?
a. 50   c. 2,000
b. 300   d. 1 million

7 True or false?
Alamosaurus was about the size of an elephant.

8 Dinosaurs laid eggs with leathery shells. The largest fossil dinosaur eggs found have a diameter of ____ inches.
a. 6 (15 cm)   c. 26 (66 cm)
b. 16 (40.6 cm)   d. 50 (127 cm)

9

True or false?

Dracorex hogwartsia was a head-butting dinosaur that was named after Draco Malfoy, an evil character in the Harry Potter books.

10

If you could travel back to prehistoric times, where might you see a pterodactyl?

a. swimming in the ocean
b. flying in the sky
c. living in a hole under the ground
d. hunting prehistoric humans

11

The name sauropod—the long-necked plant-eaters—translates to _____.

a. big bad bully
b. lizard-footed
c. sharp-toothed monster lizard
d. food-grabbing lizard

12

Why do scientists think *Troodon* was so intelligent?

a. it acted clever in *Jurassic Park*
b. it left behind stone carvings
c. it could run fast
d. it had a large brain for its body size

13

***Argentinosaurus* was likely the largest land animal ever to live on Earth. Where did the giant roam?**

a. Canada
b. South America
c. China
d. the North Pole

14

Which dinosaur had three horns and a large, bony plate behind its head?

a. *Iguanodon*
b. *Brachiosaurus*
c. *Stegosaurus*
d. *Triceratops*

15

True or false?

Many dinosaurs had feathers.

DINOSAURS OF NORTH AMERICA, 70 MILLION YEARS AGO

CHECK YOUR ANSWERS ON PAGES 167–168.

THE DIRT ON DIRT

1 If you pick up a pinch of garden soil, about how many **bacteria** are probably between your fingers?

a. dozens
b. hundreds
c. millions
d. trillions

2 True or false?
One out of every 100 atoms in Earth's crust is gold.

3 True or false?
African elephants love to take **mud** baths.

4 Erosion can break down mountains. What happens during the erosion process?

a. too many flowers grow in one place
b. water washes away soil and rock
c. lightning strikes backward
d. earthworms eat rock

5 What has been found in the soil on the planet Mars?

a. spiders
b. red plants
c. water
d. glitter

6 What do bugs, worms, bacteria, and **fungi** grind up to make new dirt?

a. dead plants and animals
b. small rocks
c. ice chunks
d. old tires

7 The **giant Gippsland** earthworm from Australia is about as long as a _____?

a. crayon
b. banana
c. baseball bat
d. school bus

Amazing SCIENCE

8 Most diamonds are formed deep in Earth's core. How do they come to the surface?

a. blasted up when asteroids strike Earth
b. washed up from the seabed by ocean currents
c. dug up by animals
d. forced up during volcanic eruptions

9 What happens most of the time when a worm gets cut in half?

a. each half grows into a new worm
b. one half survives
c. the worm explodes
d. the worm halves fight each other to the death

10 Which event most often causes mudslides?

a. lightning strikes
b. rainstorms in the mountains
c. stampeding wildebeests
d. people skiing

11 Which animal doesn't eat earthworms?

a. spiders
b. birds
c. toads
d. horses

12 Which is about the same size as a beetle mite, a common creature found in soil?

a. an atom
b. a grain of salt
c. a piece of rice
d. a grape

13 A mudpuppy spends its entire life in the water. What type of animal is it?

a. toad
b. salamander
c. dog
d. monkey

14 True or false? Some types of rocks float.

15 True or false? Scientists discovered volcanoes on Mars that spew mud.

CHECK YOUR ANSWERS ON PAGES 167–168.

GROSS OUT

1 Bacteria grow on your feet!
What do they eat to survive?
- **a.** your toenails
- **c.** fleas
- **b.** your sweat
- **d.** pizza

2 Which household object is home to
the most germs?
- **a.** a light switch
- **c.** a kitchen sponge
- **b.** a toilet seat
- **d.** a cell phone

3 True or false?
Like a fingerprint, each person's
armpit odor is unique.

4 Cave glowworms create
these strands of lights. What
material are they made of?
- **a.** tiny strands of plastic
- **b.** silk covered in sticky mucus
- **c.** the worm's barf
- **d.** bat poop

CAVE
GLOWWORMS

5 The total number of bacteria in your mouth is
closest to the human population of _____ .
- **a.** London (8 million)
- **c.** Europe (739 million)
- **b.** Japan (128 million)
- **d.** Earth (7 billion)

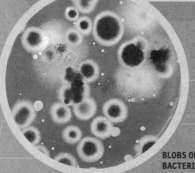

6 What does the boneless and jawless
hagfish do to escape from predators?
- **a.** lets out an explosion of gooey slime
- **b.** flashes red lights
- **c.** bites off its own tail
- **d.** disguises itself as a rock

BLOBS OF
BACTERIA

7 In early black-and-white movies, what substance was used as fake blood?

a. water and food coloring
b. vanilla pudding
c. ketchup
d. chocolate syrup

8 Which of the following is too gross for dogs to eat?

a. human poop
b. cat poop
c. their own poop
d. none of the above—some dogs love eating poop!

9 True or false?

Fungus lives in your mouth.

10 Which unsavory morsels can regularly be found in the food we eat in very small amounts?

a. maggots
b. rat hair
c. mold
d. all of the above

11 Most birds throw up food to feed their chicks. What is this process called?

a. bird barf
b. regurgitation
c. a backward gulp
d. disgust-o-snack

12 True or false?

Kangaroos never fart.

CHECK YOUR ANSWERS ON PAGES 167–168.

ECO-CHALLENGE

1 What is an **ecosystem?**

a. a 1980s video game player
b. a recycling company
c. a community of plants, animals, and their environment
d. a goat with giant, sharp teeth

2 Which insect helps almond trees produce nuts by pollinating the tree's **flowers?**

a. ant
b. honeybee
c. mosquito
d. butterfly

3 True or false? Every living creature needs **sunlight** to survive.

4 What is the leading cause of death for African **elephants?**

a. human poachers
b. old age
c. lion attacks
d. poison ivy

5 Which **ocean** animal has no natural **predators?**

a. jellyfish
b. great white shark
c. tuna
d. squid

6 What do **herbivores** eat?

a. bugs
b. rocks
c. small animals
d. plants

7 What do you call a plant or animal that shows up in an environment where it doesn't belong and causes **problems?**

a. a bully
b. an alien invader
c. an invasive species
d. the ultimate predator

8 True or false?
The white-tailed deer population in the **United States** increases during the spring.

9 Which of the following doesn't belong in a **compost pile?**

a. earthworms   c. banana peels
b. coffee grounds   d. plastic bottles

10 What are **spiders' webs** made out of?

a. plastic   c. rubber
b. silk   d. hair

11 What is a **food web?**

a. an edible spider web
b. a chart showing where animals in an environment get their energy
c. a net used to catch fish
d. a Web site where food comes from

12 True or false?
It's impossible to clean ocean waters after an oil spill.

13 Ladybugs protect plants from aphids. What are aphids?

a. a type of mushroom   c. hungry caterpillars
b. flying insects that eat leaves   d. a brand of lawnmower

AN ORB WEB SPIDER

14 What do most **plants** need to **survive?**

a. water, air, and sunlight   c. sunlight and rainbows
b. water and freezing weather   d. hamburgers and French fries

CHECK YOUR ANSWERS ON PAGES 167–168.

TRUE or FALSE?
SHAPE UP

1. IT'S IMPOSSIBLE TO KEEP A HULA-HOOP SPINNING WHILE HANGING UPSIDE DOWN.

2. A 9-YEAR-OLD GIRL OR BOY HAS TO DO 50 PUSH-UPS TO QUALIFY FOR A PRESIDENTIAL PHYSICAL FITNESS AWARD.

3. THE DISTANCE AROUND THE BASES IS THE SAME IN EVERY MAJOR LEAGUE BASEBALL FIELD.

4. A SERVING OF CHEESE PIZZA HAS ON AVERAGE MORE TOTAL FAT THAN A SERVING OF SCRAMBLED EGGS.

5. HORSES CURRENTLY COMPETE IN THE SUMMER OLYMPIC GAMES.

6. YOGA IS A HEALTHY TROPICAL FRUIT.

7. WHEN YOU GO JOGGING, YOUR BRAIN RELEASES CHEMICALS THAT MAKE YOU FEEL HAPPIER.

8. AN ASTRONAUT HAS PLAYED GOLF ON THE MOON.

9. PEOPLE WHO DON'T GET ENOUGH SLEEP TEND TO WEIGH LESS THAN PEOPLE WHO DO.

10. THE WORLD'S FASTEST TENNIS SERVE SENT A BALL ZOOMING AT 500 MILES AN HOUR (805 KM/H).

11. ZUMBA IS A TYPE OF EXERCISE THAT INVOLVES DANCING.

12. WHILE YOU SLEEP, YOUR BRAIN SHUTS OFF COMPLETELY.

13. MORE AMERICANS ARE BELIEVED TO GO RUNNING THAN BICYCLING ON ANY GIVEN DAY.

14. EATING VEGETABLES JUST ONCE A WEEK IS ENOUGH TO MAINTAIN A HEALTHY DIET.

15. PROFESSIONAL RUNNERS CAN EASILY COMPLETE A 26-MILE (41.8-KM) MARATHON IN LESS THAN 2 HOURS.

16 CHIMPANZEES CAN THROW A BALL FASTER THAN HUMAN BASEBALL PITCHERS.

17 ADULTS HAVE MORE BONES THAN BABIES DO.

18 YOU'LL LIKELY GAIN WEIGHT IF YOU DRINK TOO MUCH SUGARY SODA.

19 PURE ORANGE JUICE NATURALLY CONTAINS LOTS OF VITAMIN C.

20 REGULAR EXERCISE HELPS PREVENT HEART DISEASE.

21 JUDO IS A TEAM SPORT SIMILAR TO BASKETBALL.

22 YOUR BODY DOESN'T BURN ANY CALORIES WHILE YOU'RE VEGGING OUT ON THE SOFA.

23 PEOPLE ON A VEGAN DIET CAN EAT SCRAMBLED EGGS.

24 PEOPLE AROUND THE WORLD ON AVERAGE SPEND ABOUT 20 PERCENT OF THEIR DAY SITTING.

25 LISTENING TO MUSIC ON A JOG CAN HELP YOU RUN FARTHER.

26 WHEN YOU EXERCISE REGULARLY, ANY EXTRA FAT IN YOUR BODY TRANSFORMS INTO MUSCLE TISSUE.

27 RAW VEGETABLES ARE ALWAYS HEALTHIER THAN COOKED VEGETABLES.

28 TABLE TENNIS HAS BEEN AN OLYMPIC SPORT SINCE 1988.

29 WHEN YOU WANT TO PRACTICE BICYCLING, YOU SHOULD USE A TREADMILL.

30 THE NUMBER OF PEOPLE WHO WATCHED TV TODAY IS PROBABLY HIGHER THAN THE NUMBER WHO PLAYED A SPORT OR EXERCISED.

CHECK YOUR ANSWERS ON PAGES 167–168.

TECH TREK

1 In computer science and artificial intelligence, the Turing Test tries to determine _____ .

a. the presence of fingerprints on a computer
b. whether a computer can think
c. the number of computers in a room
d. how long a computer can last underwater

2 True or false? In the **1940s**, "computer" was a job title for people who did mathematical calculations.

3 Which animal weighs about the same as **ENIAC**, the first mechanical computer?

a. a boa constrictor
b. a grizzly bear
c. an African elephant
d. a humpback whale

4 In 2013, about what percent of the world's **7 billion** people owned a cell phone?

a. 10 percent
b. 50 percent
c. 75 percent
d. 100 percent

5 Which popular social media company came first?

a. Facebook
b. Twitter
c. YouTube
d. Instagram

6 Which technology didn't exist when Walt Disney World opened its doors to the public in 1971?

a. TV
b. cell phone
c. radio
d. space shuttle

7 Until the 1970s, what did people use to **program** computers?

a. trained monkeys
b. paper punch cards
c. voice commands
d. lasers

8 True or false?
The computers aboard the Apollo 11 moon lander were only as **powerful** as today's cell phones.

9 What technological feat did Alexander Graham Bell accomplish in **1876** in Boston, Massachusetts?
a. the first telephone call
b. the invention of the Internet
c. the discovery of electricity
d. the first funny cat video

10 *Pong* was one of the first video games. What sport was the game based on?
a. golf
b. tennis
c. soccer
d. skiing

11 True or false?
One early computer was named MANIAC.

12 **Which** of the following was the most popular hashtag on Instagram from 2010 through 2012?
a. #funny
b. #cat
c. #love
d. #lol

13 In 1997, the IBM computer Deep Blue defeated the world champion of which **game?**
a. Monopoly
b. Scrabble
c. chess
d. Angry Birds

14 In 1898, inventor **Nikola Tesla** made a boat move without touching it. How did he do it?
a. with magic
b. with hidden wires
c. with a laser pointer
d. with radio waves

15 Which of the following is about the same size as a television screen from the 1950s?
a. a postage stamp
b. a playing card
c. a magazine
d. a beach towel

CHECK YOUR ANSWERS ON PAGES 167–168.

MAD SCIENTISTS

1 What is the name of the mad scientist on *Phineas and Ferb*?

a. Dr. Dolittle
b. Maximillian Smartypants
c. Pippi Longstocking
d. Dr. Doofenshmirtz

DR. FRANKENSTEIN'S MONSTER

2 What does Dr. Frankenstein use to bring a dead body to life?

a. acid rain
b. robots
c. lightning
d. medicine

3 Which small creatures help Dr. Nefario and Felonius Gru in the movie *Despicable Me*?

a. minions
b. bugs
c. Tic Tacs
d. Beanie Babies

4 Which class did Professor Severus Snape teach at Hogwarts in the Harry Potter books?

a. history
b. potions
c. math
d. Quidditch

SEVERUS SNAPE

5 Which movie features robots named C-3PO and R2-D2?

a. *Toy Story*
b. *The Incredibles*
c. *Ice Age*
d. *Star Wars*

C-3PO

6 What strange physical feature does Mr. Crocker from *The Fairly OddParents* have?

a. two thumbs on each hand
b. blue skin
c. ears on his neck
d. missing eyebrows

R2-D2

DOCTOR OCTOPUS

7 Mad scientist Doctor Octopus is the nemesis of which superhero?

a. Superman
b. Batman
c. Spider-Man
d. Catwoman

8 The evil genius Plankton is a character in which TV show?

a. *SpongeBob SquarePants*
b. *Phineas and Ferb*
c. *Looney Tunes*
d. *The Powerpuff Girls*

9 In the cartoon *Dexter's Laboratory*, who always manages to get into the boy genius's secret lab?

a. his sister, Dee Dee
b. an intelligent elephant
c. his parents
d. government agents

10 Beetee, an electronics and wiring whiz, allies with Katniss Everdeen in which book?

a. *Percy Jackson & The Olympians: The Sea of Monsters*
b. *Harry Potter and the Chamber of Secrets*
c. *The Hunger Games: Catching Fire*
d. *Diary of a Wimpy Kid*

11 In the movie *Spy Kids: All the Time in the World*, mad scientist Danger D'Amo's name is an anagram for _____.

a. famous Amos
b. Armageddon
c. dragon-man
d. doctor mango

12 In the cartoon *Johnny Test*, who performs science experiments on Johnny?

a. aliens
b. his older sisters
c. secret government agents
d. an intelligent octopus

A MAD SCIENTIST

CHECK YOUR ANSWERS ON PAGES 167–168.

ANIMAL Name Game

1 After which cartoon character was a new species of mushroom named?

a. Bugs Bunny
b. Ferb Fletcher
c. SpongeBob SquarePants
d. Bart Simpson

2 What is this animal's name?

a. no no
b. aye-aye
c. bug-eyes
d. Bubba

COBRA

3 *Bittium* is the scientific name of a small marine snail. What is its even smaller relative named?

a. Teensy-weensy
b. Little *bittium*
c. Mini-snail
d. *Ittibittium*

4 True or false?
A group of cobras is called a quiver.

DUGONG

5 Which animal is this dugong most closely related to?

a. elephant
b. shark
c. seal
d. tortoise

6 For $650,000, a Web site bought the rights to name a newly discovered species of monkey. How was the money used?

a. to fund a castle as the monkeys' home
b. as hidden treasure
c. it was donated to charity
d. it got stolen

Amazing SCIENCE

7 Which of the following is not a real animal?
a. pink fairy armadillo   c. flying shark cat
b. blobfish   d. dumbo octopus

8 If you come across a skulk, what group of sneaky animals have you found?
a. rabbits   c. foxes
b. polar bears   d. flamingos

GREATER FLAMINGO

9 Why is this creature called the yeti crab?
a. it looks like a monster
b. it's the size of a gorilla
c. it has long, hairy arms
d. it lives in snowy mountains

10 The Darth Vader beetle is named after the villain from which movie?
a. *Star Wars*   c. *Spy Kids*
b. *The Lion King*   d. *Star Trek*

SUCKER-FOOTED BAT

11 Which of the following is the scientific name of a type of beetle that eats jelly-like slime molds?
a. Gelae donut   c. Jelly monster
b. Slime attack   d. all of the above

12 True or false?
The sucker-footed bat uses the force of suction on its feet to cling to leaves.

13 What's the word for a group of porcupines?
a. ball   c. slam dunk
b. prickle   d. herd

PORCUPINE

GAME SHOW

ULTIMATE SCIENCE CHALLENGE

1 What did a *Triceratops* mostly eat?
- **a.** birds
- **b.** plants
- **c.** fish
- **d.** all of the above

2 TRUE OR FALSE?
You have more bones in both your feet than in the rest of your body.

3 What should you do if you find an earthworm in your garden?
- **a.** put it out in the sun
- **b.** squash it
- **c.** give it to birds for breakfast
- **d.** leave it there—it's good for the soil!

5 TRUE OR FALSE?
Researchers have built a computer that is smaller than a penny.

4 Plankton, an important part of the ocean food web, are _____.
- **a.** very tiny plants and animals
- **b.** seaweeds
- **c.** wrecked pirate ships
- **d.** mermaid scales

7 On average, how much longer does your hair grow each year?
- **a.** 1 inch (2.5 cm)
- **b.** 6 inches (15 cm)
- **c.** 1 foot (30.5 cm)
- **d.** 2 feet (61 cm)

6 Which Australian bird has a call that sounds like laughter?
- **a.** haha bird
- **b.** kookaburra
- **c.** doofus
- **d.** pineapple

8 If you microwave a bean seed for 5 minutes, the seed will _____.

a. explode
b. start to sprout
c. release a smell like dirty socks
d. fail to grow

9 Which cartoon features an evil boy scientist named Mandark?

a. *Dexter's Laboratory*
b. *SpongeBob SquarePants*
c. *The Fairly OddParents*
d. *Johnny Test*

10 TRUE OR FALSE?

Some pinecones are male and others are female.

11 Which animal sleeps standing up?

a.
ostrich

c.
hippo

b.
jaguar

d.
horse

12 What symbols does a computer use to store information?

a. 1 and 0
b. triangles and squares
c. gold and silver stars
d. A, B, and C

13 TRUE OR FALSE?

Skunk spray often kills foxes and coyotes.

14 The Great Pacific Garbage Patch is a floating mass of stuff in the middle of the ocean made up mostly of _____.

a. candy wrappers
b. banana peels
c. tiny pieces of plastic
d. seahorses

15 ULTIMATE BRAIN BUSTER

What was this dial used for in the past?

a. playing music
b. paying for groceries
c. making phone calls
d. locating submarines

CAMPING ON MER DE GLACE
GLACIER, FRANCE

Climbing MOUNT EVEREST

1 Mount Everest is named after Sir George Everest, who was _____.
a. the first person to climb Mount Everest
b. a surveyor who mapped the Himalaya mountains
c. a famous snowboarder
d. a Chinese king

CLIMBERS APPROACH THE SUMMIT OF MOUNT EVEREST

2 Mount Everest is the world's tallest mountain. How tall is it?
a. 9,035 feet (2,754 m)
b. 19,035 feet (5,802 m)
c. 29,035 feet (8,850 m)
d. 39,035 feet (11,898 m)

3 Sherpas—a group of people who live in the Himalaya—are frequently hired as _____ by Mount Everest climbers.
a. guides
b. cooks
c. doctors
d. performers

4 If you hear a group of sherpas say *Chomolungma*, they mean _____.
a. "Look out—avalanche!"
b. "base camp"
c. "Mount Everest"
d. "Let's eat!"

A SHERPA

5 Which of the following is not a risk faced by climbers on Everest?
a. sunburned eyes
b. falling
c. lack of oxygen
d. Siberian tiger attack

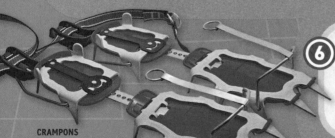

CRAMPONS

6 Tools called crampons help climbers to do what?
a. navigate
b. move on snow and ice
c. keep warm
d. communicate

7 In 1998, French climber Jean-Marc Boivin descended from the summit of Mount Everest in only 11 minutes of _____.

a. snowboarding   c. hang gliding
b. paragliding   d. tubing

8 Which country can you see from the mountain's summit?

a. India   c. Nepal
b. Tibet   d. all of the above

9 Which animal would you never encounter around Mount Everest?

a. red panda   c. bald eagle
b. snow leopard   d. Himalayan black bear

SNOW LEOPARD

10 True or false?
Sir Edmund Hillary, one of the first to climb Mount Everest, led an expedition to find a snow monster called a Yeti.

11 As you scale the peak, you'll reach the "Death Zone," an area of Everest where _____.

a. there is very little oxygen
b. the most crevasses occur
c. climbers have snowball fights
d. many predatory animals live

CARTOON YETI

12 What is one way to warm up frostbitten fingers?

a. stick them in your armpits
b. wear damp gloves
c. build a snowman
d. wave them in the air

13 In 2011, 8 tons of _____ was removed from Mount Everest.

a. snow   c. rock
b. trash   d. dirt

GALAXY QUEST

1 What did astronaut John Young get in trouble for in **1962**?

a. not wearing a seat belt while in flight
b. blasting off before the countdown was complete
c. sneaking a corned beef sandwich onto the spacecraft
d. putting mission control on hold while he answered another call

3 Which of the following have robotic rovers on **Mars** discovered?

a. Martians   c. plants
b. an ancient streambed   d. fossilized insects

5 Which cartoon character is **NASA's** safety mascot?

a. Sandy Cheeks   c. Scooby-Doo
b. Snoopy   d. Bart Simpson

2 True or false? The Apollo astronauts who landed on the moon all claimed that moondust smelled like **cheese**.

4 In China, people who are trained for spaceflight are called _____.

a. astronauts   c. cosmonauts
b. taikonauts   d. spacionauts

6 True or false? A dummy named Ivan Ivanovich was blasted into orbit for a Soviet Union (U.S.S.R.) test flight in early 1961.

7 What is the hottest planet in the solar system?

a. Mercury   c. Earth
b. Venus   d. Mars

8 The word "**comet**" comes from a Greek word that means _____.

a. wearing long hair   c. fuzzy
b. space invader   d. yogurt

9 True or false?
The space shuttle *Discovery* was named after a pirate ship.

10 Which of the following **planets** does not have rings?

a. Mercury   c. Jupiter
b. Saturn   d. Neptune

11 In which part of our solar system is **Pluto** located?

a. the asteroid belt
b. the Andromeda galaxy
c. the Kuiper belt
d. the Virgo cluster

12 Which planet is named after the **Roman** god of the sea?

a. Mercury   c. Jupiter
b. Mars   d. Neptune

13 Approximately how long does it take for light from the sun to reach **Earth**?

a. 8.3 minutes   c. 8.3 days
b. 8.3 hours   d. 8.3 years

THE MILKY WAY

14 What created the "happy face" image on the surface of **Mars**?

a. a lake   c. a crater
b. aliens   d. nothing, it's an illusion

SAMURAI WARRIORS

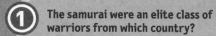

1 The samurai were an elite class of warriors from which country?

a. Mexico   **c.** China
b. Japan   **d.** Norway

2 If a samurai was fighting an enemy, which of the following weapons might he use?

a. bow and arrow   **c.** sword
b. lance   **d.** all of the above

3 The Marvel comic book character Silver Samurai is known for his sharp clashes with what well-known hero?

a. Spider-Man   **c.** the Incredible Hulk
b. Wolverine   **d.** Captain America

4 The samurai followed a code of conduct called _____.

a. the Bill of Rights   **c.** Bushido
b. chivalry   **d.** Morse Code

SAMURAI AND HIS HORSE

5 According to this code, the samurai had to remain loyal to his _____.

a. servants
b. horse
c. master
d. accountant

CARTOON SAMURAI

6 The word "samurai" means one who _____.

a. serves   **c.** skates
b. dances   **d.** fights

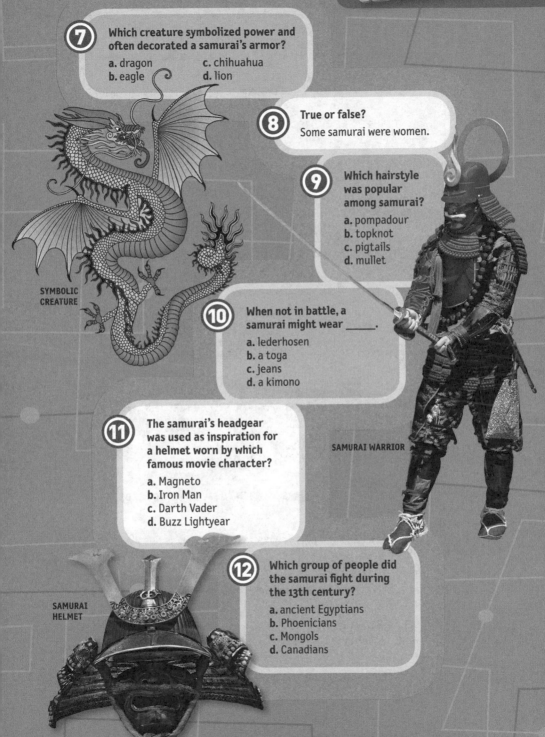

7 Which creature symbolized power and often decorated a samurai's armor?
a. dragon
b. eagle
c. chihuahua
d. lion

8 True or false?
Some samurai were women.

9 Which hairstyle was popular among samurai?
a. pompadour
b. topknot
c. pigtails
d. mullet

SYMBOLIC CREATURE

10 When not in battle, a samurai might wear _____.
a. lederhosen
b. a toga
c. jeans
d. a kimono

SAMURAI WARRIOR

11 The samurai's headgear was used as inspiration for a helmet worn by which famous movie character?
a. Magneto
b. Iron Man
c. Darth Vader
d. Buzz Lightyear

SAMURAI HELMET

12 Which group of people did the samurai fight during the 13th century?
a. ancient Egyptians
b. Phoenicians
c. Mongols
d. Canadians

CHECK YOUR ANSWERS ON PAGES 169–170.

TRUE or FALSE?
Famous Explorations

1 EARLY SPANISH EXPLORERS WHO CONQUERED PARTS OF THE AMERICAS IN THE 16TH CENTURY WERE CALLED CONQUISTADORS.

2 ROALD DAHL WAS THE FIRST EXPLORER TO REACH THE SOUTH POLE.

3 CHINESE EXPLORER ZHENG HAD VEGETABLE GARDENS ON HIS SHIPS TO FEED HIS CREW WHEN THEY EXPLORED THE INDIAN OCEAN IN THE 15TH CENTURY.

4 IN 2012, A UKRANIAN CAVER DESCENDED A CAVE THAT IS DEEPER THAN THE HEIGHT OF FOUR STACKED EMPIRE STATE BUILDINGS.

5 PORTUGUESE EXPLORER VASCO DA GAMA INSPIRED THE NAME OF A BRAZILIAN SOCCER TEAM.

6 NATIVE AMERICAN POCAHONTAS MARRIED CAPTAIN JOHN SMITH.

7 ENGLISH EXPLORER HENRY HUDSON REPORTED A MERMAID SIGHTING NEAR NORWAY.

8 THE SPACECRAFT THAT EXPLORED VENUS IN THE 1990S WAS NAMED AFTER EXPLORER FERDINAND MAGELLAN, WHO LED THE TRIP TO CIRCUMNAVIGATE THE GLOBE IN 1519.

9 VIKING LEIF ERIKSON MOST LIKELY DISCOVERED CANADA BY ACCIDENT 500 YEARS BEFORE COLUMBUS ARRIVED IN NORTH AMERICA.

10 AVIATOR AMELIA EARHART WAS THE FIRST PERSON TO FLY NONSTOP ACROSS THE ATLANTIC OCEAN.

11 THE ANCIENT GREEKS WERE THE FIRST PEOPLE TO USE A COMPASS FOR NAVIGATION.

12 EARLY EXPLORERS REFERRED TO NORTH AND SOUTH AMERICA AS THE "OLD WORLD."

13 AFTER DISCOVERING NOODLES IN CHINA, MARCO POLO INTRODUCED PASTA TO ITALY WHEN HE RETURNED TO HIS HOME COUNTRY IN 1295.

14 U.S. PRESIDENT THEODORE ROOSEVELT WAS ONE OF THE FIRST PEOPLE TO MAP THE AMAZON RIVER.

15 MERIWETHER LEWIS AND WILLIAM CLARK ARE OFTEN CREDITED WITH DISCOVERING THE NORTH POLE.

16 U.S. PRESIDENT BENJAMIN HARRISON MADE COLUMBUS DAY AN OFFICIAL HOLIDAY IN 1892.

17 SOME HISTORIANS BELIEVE THAT SPANISH EXPLORER PONCE DE LEÓN DISCOVERED FLORIDA IN 1513 WHILE SEARCHING FOR THE FOUNTAIN OF YOUTH.

18 OCEANOGRAPHER SYLVIA EARLE CANNOT SWIM.

19 VIKINGS SOMETIMES USED CROWS TO HELP THEM NAVIGATE ON FOGGY DAYS.

20 MOVIEMAKER JAMES CAMERON DISCOVERED THE R.M.S. *TITANIC* SHIPWRECK.

21 *ALVIN*, A FAMOUS SUBMERSIBLE USED TO EXPLORE DEEP-OCEAN ENVIRONMENTS, WAS NAMED AFTER ALVIN THE CHIPMUNK.

22 A CAVE FULL OF GIANT CRYSTALS WAS DISCOVERED IN MEXICO IN 2000.

23 IN 2001, POLAR EXPLORERS ANN BANCROFT AND LIV ARNESEN CROSSED ANTARCTICA USING SKIS AND SAILS.

24 IT TOOK ADVENTURER STEVE FOSSETT LESS THAN 15 DAYS TO TRAVEL AROUND THE WORLD IN A HOT-AIR BALLOON IN THE SUMMER OF 2002.

25 BEFORE ABOUT 1800, MANY SAILORS DIED FROM SCURVY BECAUSE THEY DIDN'T HAVE FRESH FRUITS AND VEGETABLES AT SEA.

26 ENGLISH EXPLORER SIR FRANCIS DRAKE WAS CONSIDERED A PIRATE BY SOME PEOPLE.

27 ITALIAN EXPLORER CHRISTOPHER COLUMBUS AND HIS CREW INVENTED THE HAMMOCK.

28 SACAGAWEA, WHO ACCOMPANIED THE LEWIS AND CLARK EXPEDITION WEST OF THE MISSISSIPPI RIVER, IS THE ONLY WOMAN TO APPEAR ON A U.S. COIN.

29 ITALIAN MERCHANT MARCO POLO SPENT 24 YEARS TRAVELING FROM EUROPE TO ASIA.

30 THE ORIGINAL NAME OF COLUMBUS'S SHIP *LA NIÑA* WAS *SANTA CLARA*.

CAMP THRILLS

2 The log cabin, the star, and the reflector are **types of** ____.
a. campfire designs
b. tents
c. camp counselors
d. constellations

1 **Which pesky plant has given many campgoers an itch they can't seem to scratch?**
a. Venus flytrap
b. Saguaro cactus
c. poison ivy
d. daisy

3 **Which popular campfire snack received an official entry in the Merriam-Webster dictionary in 1974?**
a. hot dog   c. s'more
b. marshmallow   d. salad

4 **Clove hitch, square, and bowline are all types of** ____.
a. dance moves   c. insect repellents
b. plants   d. knots

5 **True or false? Adults are more prone to getting mosquito bites than kids.**

6 **In 2013, many campers used Rainbow Loom to create bracelets made from which material?**
a. string   c. shells
b. rubber bands   d. spaghetti

7 **Which of the following water activities is not an Olympic sport?**
a. canoeing   c. rowing
b. swimming   d. water-skiing

8 The **French** version of the game leapfrog is called *saute-mouton*, which means _____.

a. frog legs
b. lily pad
c. hip hop
d. leap sheep

9 True or false?
At one summer camp in Massachusetts, kids and teens must battle **zombies**.

10 What material did the ancient Romans use to make their **tents?**

a. cotton
b. leather
c. cheese
d. plastic

11 How do you safely put out a campfire?

a. pour water over it until the embers stop burning
b. cover it with a blanket
c. shovel dirt over it until the embers stop burning
d. either a or c

12 Which of the following is a **strap** made by braiding pieces of cord?

a. fishing line
b. lanyard
c. topknot
d. pigtails

13 In 2002, more than 2,000 people gathered in Zwolle, Netherlands, to participate in which popular summer-camp **game?**

a. sack race
b. capture the flag
c. tug-of-war
d. hide-and-seek

14 The main action of which of the following movies does *not* take place in a camp?

a. *The Parent Trap*
b. *Camp Rock 2: The Final Jam*
c. *Cloudy With a Chance of Meatballs*
d. *Race for Your Life, Charlie Brown*

MAP MANIA!
DIG IT UP!

Dig this! Scientists have traveled the world searching for the fossils of dinosaurs and other prehistoric creatures. Answer these questions to test your knowledge about these dynamite discoveries.

ARCTIC OCEAN

NORTH AMERICA

H

B

ATLANTIC OCEAN

SOUTH AMERICA

PACIFIC OCEAN

F

D

GIANT HUMAN

ARCHAEOPTERYX

1 ENGLAND

True or false?

After the fossil bone of a *Megalosaurus* was found in England in 1676, an Oxford University professor mistakenly identified it as a giant human.

2 GERMANY

From fossils of the feathered dinosaur *Archaeopteryx*, scientists concluded that the creature was able to_____.

a. swim   **c.** run
b. fly   **d.** swim and fly

3 ANTARCTICA

Scientists in Antarctica discovered the full fossil of a reptile called a *Plesiosaur*, which had four fins and likely lived _____.

a. in the mountains   **c.** on a beach
b. on an ice sheet   **d.** in the water

4 UNITED STATES

Scientists believe that this dinosaur skull discovered in Montana, U.S.A., in 2007 belonged to which large meat-eater?

a. *Tyrannosaurus rex*
b. *Triceratops*
c. *Apatosaurus*
d. *Eodromaeus*

PLESIOSAUR

5 SOUTH AFRICA

Examination of fossil skulls of the dinosaur *Massospondylus* shows a pair of large "nares" and a pair of large "orbits." These indicate the animal had good senses of ____ .

a. touch and sight
b. smell and sight
c. smell and taste
d. touch and taste

MASSOSPONDYLUS

6 ALGERIA

This fossil tooth is from a North African dinosaur, *Carcharodontosaurus*. The creature lived during ____.

a. the Triassic period
b. the Cretaceous period
c. the Middle Ages
d. the Industrial Age

CARCHARODONTOSAURUS TOOTH

ARGENTINOSAURUS

7 MONGOLIA

The *Velociraptor*, which was first discovered in 1923, was named for which feature?

d. its meat-eating abilities
b. its large brain
c. its sharp teeth
d. its speed

8 ARGENTINA

Argentinosaurus, whose fossils were first found in 1993, was a giant plant-eater that belonged to a group of dinosaurs called ____.

a. sauropods
b. theropods
c. cerapods
d. carnivores

VELOCIRAPTOR

9–16 RED DOTS ON THE MAP MARK WHERE EACH CREATURE WAS DISCOVERED. MATCH EACH FOSSIL TO THE PLACE OF ITS DISCOVERY.

EUROPE
ASIA
E
A
AFRICA
PACIFIC OCEAN
INDIAN OCEAN
AUSTRALIA
G

GAME SHOW
ULTIMATE ADVENTURE CHALLENGE

1 Daredevil Evel Knievel did not jump his motorcycle over _____.
a. 50 stacked cars
b. a shark tank
c. 14 buses
d. a crate of rattlesnakes

2 TRUE OR FALSE?
The world's tallest roller coaster, Zumanjaro: Drop of Doom, is taller than the Statue of Liberty.

3 TRUE OR FALSE?
Vikings wore horned helmets in battle.

4 Which pirate's ship was discovered off the coast of North Carolina?
a. Calico Jack   c. Blackbeard
b. William Kidd   d. Captain Hook

5 The plates on the back of a *Stegosaurus* were used _____.
a. as radiators   c. to attract mates
b. as signals   d. all of the above

6 On which of these waterways can you go white-water rafting?
a. Colorado River   c. Yangtze River
b. Nile River   d. all of the above

7 In 2013, more than 200,000 people applied to be part of a mission to one day colonize which planet?
a. Venus   c. Jupiter
b. Mars   d. Neptune

9 TRUE OR FALSE?
There are mountains taller than Mount Everest under the ocean.

8 In the 1920s, daredevils who performed stunts on the wings of planes were often called _____.
a. flappers   c. athletes
b. barnstormers   d. pilots

11 Which of the following cowboys was not an outlaw in the American Wild West?
a. Butch Cassidy   c. Buffalo Bill
b. Jesse James   d. Billy the Kid

10 Which of the following adventure stories takes place on the Mississippi River?
a. *The Swiss Family Robinson*
b. *Treasure Island*
c. *Adventures of Huckleberry Finn*
d. *Journey to the Center of the Earth*

12 Stories of Robin Hood usually take place in what forest?
a. Redwood Forest
b. Western Woods
c. Sherwood Forest
d. the Enchanted Forest

13 On what reality television show are contestants forced to live in a remote area and compete for food?
a. *The Amazing Race*
b. *Survivor*
c. *Dancing With the Stars*
d. *Win, Lose, or Draw*

14 **ULTIMATE BRAIN BUSTER** What gift from elementary school students did American astronaut Alan Shepard carry to space in 1961?

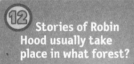 a. cupcakes

b. a toy spaceship

 c. a tie

 d. an American flag

CHECK YOUR ANSWERS ON PAGES 169–170.

ANSWERS

Animal QUEST

Life's a Zoo, pages 10–11

1. d   2. c   3. a
4. **True.** The population of wild tigers is estimated at about 3,000, while 15,000 to 20,000 tigers live in captivity.
5. d   6. c   7. b   8. b
9. **False.** Female lions hunt more than male lions do. They work together to bring down prey.
10. d
11. **False.** James is 6 feet 8 inches (2 m) tall, and most giraffes' legs are 6 feet (1.9 m) long.
12. a

Escape Artists, pages 12–13

1. c   2. a   3. b
4. **True.** Scientists believe that communication rather than camouflage is the main purpose of chameleons' flashy color changes.
5. a   6. d   7. a   8. b   9. a
10. **False.** A sweet scent lures insects into the pitcher plant, where they drown in a pool of water.
11. b

Freaky Frogs, pages 14–15

1. **False.** The frog sleeps with its eyes closed, and flashes them open when startled.
2. **True.** A frog's eyeballs sink down into its head while swallowing. This helps move the food down its throat.
3. b   4. c   5. b   6. b
7. **True.** The golden poison arrow dart frog is one of the most toxic animals.
8. a   9. a   10. d   11. d
12. c   13. a   14. b
15. **False.** The African clawed frog has no tongue.

Lights Out! Animals at Night, pages 16–17

1. a   2. c   3. b
4. **True.** Cats' eyes have a special light-reflecting surface that helps them see better at night.
5. b   6. a   7. a
8. **False.** Moths trying to use the moon's light to navigate get confused and disoriented by electric lights.
9. c   10. d   11. c   12. a
13. **False.** Night monkeys, bush babies, and several lemur and loris species are nocturnal.

True or False? Creature Features, pages 18–19

1. **True.** Butterflies can see colors in the ultraviolet spectrum that are beyond human vision.
2. **False.** Pelicans use the pouch to catch fish, and then they swallow the fish right away.
3. **True.** Tapirs are related to the horse and rhinoceros, and live in the rainforests of South America and Malaysia.
4. **True.** The paste comes from a scent pouch located beneath the hyena's tail.
5. **True.** The mantis shrimp can strike faster than a .22-caliber bullet.
6. **True.** Green sea turtles crawl up onto the beach and use their flippers like shovels to dig a nest in the sand.
7. **False.** Great white sharks can sense blood in the water up to about 3 miles (4.8 km) away.
8. **False.** Dolphins and whales are mammals, and they have two flippers and a tail. Also, humans have two legs and two arms!
9. **False.** The Bactrian camel, from Mongolia, has two humps, while the dromedary, from Africa and the Middle East, has one.
10. **True.** In an experiment at the University of Oxford, Betty bent a piece of wire and used the hook to get food.
11. **True.** Penguins evolved to be fantastic swimmers, but their wings won't carry them through the air.
12. **False.** You won't die instantly, but you could get the disease rabies, which is almost always deadly if not treated.
13. **False.** The spider monkey uses its long tail like another arm to help it swing through branches and hold on to things.
14. **True.** The anaconda's jawbones can easily move apart to allow the mouth to stretch wide open.
15. **False.** Jaguars are good swimmers, and often eat frogs, fish, and turtles.
16. **True.** Snow leopards live in the mountains of Central Asia, where the weather can get very cold.
17. **True.** A group of sea otters floating together is called a raft.
18. **True.** All birds have feathers, even penguins!
19. **False.** Wallace's flying frog lives in the jungles of Malaysia and Borneo, and uses its large, webbed feet to glide through the air.
20. **False.** Fireflies create their own light with a special organ.
21. **True.** Penguins, ducks, and polar bears all have webbed feet.
22. **False.** Herons eat fish, and use their sharp beak like a spear to catch prey.
23. **True.** One ostrich eye is about 2 inches (5 cm) across.
24. **True.** The kookaburra is a bird native to Australia.
25. **True.** The electric eel can generate 600 volts, while a standard U.S.A. wall socket is just 110–120 volts.
26. **False.** Many snakes, including the brown water snake and corn snake, are not venomous.
27. **True.** A colony of naked mole rats has a single queen and worker rats.
28. **True.** Sea turtles can safely eat box jellyfish, but humans can die from contact with their venomous tentacles.
29. **False.** Polar bears live around the North Pole, and penguins live near the South Pole.
30. **False.** Skunk spray is smelly and uncomfortable, but not deadly.

Animal Feats!, pages 20–21

1. c
2. **True.** Some species of rhinoceros beetle can lift things 850 times their own weight!
3. b   4. c   5. d   6. d   7. c
8. **True.** The arctic tern migrates from the North Pole to the South Pole and back each year!
9. a   10. d   11. a
12. **True.** Flying fish can reach heights of more than 4 feet (1.2 m) and can glide for 655 feet (200 m).

Map Mania! Back From the Brink, pages 22–23

1. L   2. J   3. K   4. I   5. H
6. G   7. F   8. E   9. B   10. D
11. C   12. A

Panda-Monium, pages 24–25

1. c   2. c   3. d
4. **False.** The American black bear can walk on its hind legs, but the giant panda can't do this.

5. **b**
6. **False.** Panda bears in the zoo eat bamboo, but also rice gruel, sugar cane, carrots, apples, and sweet potatoes.
7. **a**
8. **True.** Panda bears develop black markings as they grow up.
9. **d**   10. **b**   11. **d**
12. **True.** Pandas have a long wrist bone that works like a thumb to grasp and hold bamboo.
13. **a**   14. **c**   15. **b**

Kidding Around, pages 26–27
1. **d**
2. **False.** Most motorcycles weigh about 400 to 500 pounds (181 to 227 kg), while a baby elephant weighs about 200 pounds (91 kg) at birth.
3. **a**   4. **c**   5. **b**

6. **True**
7. **a**   8. **c**   9. **c**
10. **False.** Caribou calves grow antlers as they get older.
11. **a**   12. **b**
13. **d**   14. **b**

Dating Game, pages 28–29
1. **d**   2. **b**
3. **True.** A male spider is more likely to get eaten if he's much smaller than the female.
4. **a**   5. **b**   6. **b**
7. **True.** Whiptail lizards reproduce through cloning.
8. **a**   9. **b**
10. **a**   11. **b**
12. **False.** A female chameleon changes to bright colors to keep males away when she's not ready to mate.

Game Show: Ultimate Animal Challenge, pages 30–31
1. **d**
2. **True.** The giant river otter is an endangered species native to the Amazon rain forest.
3. **d**   4. **b**   5. **b**   6. **c**
7. **False.** Panda bears are good swimmers.
8. **b**   9. **a**   10. **d**
11. **c.** The narwhal's horn is actually its left front tooth!
12. **a**   13. **c**   14. **c**
15. **Monarch**

SCORING

0–54

GETTING STARTED
You might not be able to tell a fish from a frog or a lobster from a crab now, but if you take a trip to the local zoo or aquarium, you'll be on your way to expanding your mind with animal expertise.

55–108

MIND OVER MANATEE!
You're smarter than the manatee, and could match wits with a brainy dolphin. You love creatures so much, you probably have animal posters all over your room!

109–161

A WHALE OF A BRAIN!
Your brain must be as big as a whale's, and packed full of knowledge. You may grow up to be a marine biologist, veterinarian, or zookeeper!

Globe TROTTING

Say What!, pages 34–35
1. **True**
2. **c**   3. **b**   4. **a**
5. **c** ("pneumonoultramicroscopicsilicovolcanoconiosis"—a lung disease)
6. **b**   7. **a**   8. **b**
9. **False.** It means chattering of teeth.
10. **b**   11. **c**   12. **a**   13. **c**

Ends of the Earth, pages 36–37
1. **b**
2. **False.** Polar bears live in the Arctic region; penguins live in the Southern Hemisphere, especially in Antarctica.
3. **a**

4. **True**
5. **d**   6. **b**
7. **False.** Blue is another common color, but they can also be green, red, gray, brown, or black!
8. **a**   9. **b**   10. **c**   11. **b**   12. **b**
13. **c**   14. **d**
15. **True.** This is due to the tilt of Earth's axis. And in the winter at the poles, the sun never rises!

There's No Place Like Home, pages 38–39
1. **b**   2. **True**   3. **a**   4. **c**   5. **b**
6. **c**   7. **b**   8. **b**   9. **a**
10. **True**   11. **c**   12. **False**

What's for Dinner?, pages 40–41
1. **True.** About 2 billion people eat 1,400 different species of insects, spiders, and crustaceans.
2. **c**   3. **a**   4. **c**   5. **b**
6. **False.** Food is only eaten with the right hand, as the left hand is considered unclean.
7. **a**   8. **b**   9. **b**   10. **a**   11. **b**
12. **c**
13. **True.** For people to use separate plates is considered silly.

True or False? Where in the World?, pages 42–43

1. **True.** For a long time Iran was in the lead, but in recent years the U.S.A. has challenged them.
2. **False.** The Wall is about 13,170 miles (21,195 km) long, while Australia's coastline is a little more than 16,000 miles (25,750 km) long.
3. **True.** On average, each person earns more than $88,000 a year.
4. **False.** That temperature is the highest ever recorded but it was in the U.S.A., in Furnace Creek Ranch, CA, on July 10, 1913.
5. **True.** It happened on July 21, 1983.
6. **True.** There is a major network of bike paths in the Netherlands.
7. **False.** The Amazon is the largest river (most water), but at 4,135 miles (6,655 km), the Nile in Africa is longer.
8. **True.** There are four islands but only the one named Pitcairn has people on it.
9. **False.** The oldest known prehuman fossils have been found in a section of Africa including Ethiopia, Kenya, Uganda, and Tanzania.
10. **True.** His name was Tadeusz Kosciuszko.
11. **False.** Prior to the 2014 World Cup, Brazil had won five times and Italy had won four.
12. **True.** It means "How are you?"
13. **True.** Canada has at least two million lakes—and possibly more than three million.
14. **False.** Soccer is the number one sport for both boys and girls.
15. **False.** That honor goes to China.
16. **True.** Last names in Iceland are based on your father's first name.
17. **True**
18. **False.** It means rain.
19. **True.** It's for good luck.
20. **False.** It is a popular dish in that country.
21. **True.** The 10-day Boryeong Mud Festival held in summer is popular among teenagers and adults.
22. **True.** He received the patent in 1846.
23. **False.** It was Isabel Perón in Argentina in 1974.
24. **True.** It is the Museum of Microminiatures in Kiev.
25. **True.** "El Apóstol" by Quirino Cristiani was made in 1917.
26. **False.** Actually, holding up your open palm with fingers extended is a serious insult!
27. **False.** There are not really any mountains in the country.
28. **True.** They also make antelope masks.
29. **True.** It is two overlapping triangles.
30. **False.** It is actually a magic mouse with different names in Latin American countries, such as Ratoncito.

Lucky Charms, pages 44–45

1. b   2. **True**   3. a   4. b   5. a
6. **True.** But tradition there also says you will be punished if you kill a vulture.
7. **False.** It is especially popular in Turkey.
8. a   9. d
10. **True.** They believe frogs bring the rain.

Back to School, pages 46–47

1. **True.** Girls enter, then boys, all stand at desks, teacher greets them, students reply, then they sit.
2. b   3. **False**   4. a   5. b
6. b   7. c
8. **False.** Students stand when the teacher enters.
9. c   10. c   11. c   12. a   13. b
14. **True.** The boat picks up about 30 students at their homes, they have classes, and are dropped off later.

Map Mania! Roadside Attractions, pages 48–49

1. d   2. d   3. b   4. c   5. a
6. b   7. c   8. 1F   9. 2D   10. 3B
11. 4G   12. 5C   13. 6E   14. 7A

Game Show: Ultimate Global Challenge, pages 50–51

1. a
2. **False.** The seasons are reversed. So in September, when there is the least ice in the Arctic, there is the most ice in Antarctica.
3. c   4. a
5. **False.** They originated in South America.
6. c   7. b   8. b   9. b   10. c
11. c
12. **True.** Guests are also expected to eat first and to eat the most food.
13. c   14. d   15. a

SCORING

0–44

OFF THE BEATEN TRACK!

There's lots to discover in your own backyard and local neighborhood. Having explored these, go off-road with your family and investigate the natural landscape. You'll learn about the wider world and may get the desire to travel the world.

45–88

ALL SHIP-SHAPE!

Now that you have your sea legs, you are ready to set sail. You have got the travel bug and are ready to explore far and wide. So pack your bags with clothes, guidebook, compass, camera, and binoculars and get out there and discover Earth's treasures.

89–136

OUT OF THIS WORLD!

You plan to journey on a globe-trotting tour, visiting as many countries as you can. You want to learn about different cultures and societies, try different foods, and see weird and wonderful places. And when you have completed your journey, you'll have your heart set on space travel.

Pop CULTURE

Channel Surfing, pages 54–55

1. b
2. **True.** The television show *Dog With a Blog* is about a dog named Stan who writes a blog.
3. d   4. c   5. b   6. b   7. a
8. b   9. a   10. d   11. d   12. b
13. **True.** The members of the band auditioned separately for the U.K. version of the show, but the judges suggested they form a group.

Super Sidekicks, pages 56–57

1. b   2. a   3. a   4. d   5. a
6. c   7. c   8. a   9. b   10. b
11. c   12. b   13. a

True or False? It's Showtime!, pages 58–59

1. **True.** Constantine looks exactly like Kermit the Frog, but unlike Kermit, he is a criminal.
2. **False.** The movies have taken place in North America, Africa, and Europe.
3. **True.** Agent J travels back in time to stop an alien from assassinating a young Agent K.
4. **True.** King Fergus gives Merida bows and arrows for her sixth birthday.
5. **False.** Loki morphs into Captain America.
6. **False.** Gargamel creates a pair of Smurf-like characters called the Naughties.
7. **False.** Wreck-It Ralph is the villain of a video game called *Fix-It Felix, Jr.*
8. **False.** Mavis, who is Dracula's daughter, celebrates her 118th birthday in the movie.
9. **False.** Maleficent casts a spell on Princess Aurora, otherwise known as "Sleeping Beauty."
10. **False.** Gwen Stacy's father is police officer Captain George Stacy.
11. **False.** Tonto is a Comanche Indian.
12. **True.** Metro Man lies about copper draining his power because he no longer wants to be a hero.
13. **True.** In addition to Sonic the Hedgehog, the movie features other classic video game characters such as Q*Bert, Bowser, and Doctor Eggman.
14. **True.** Indiana's fear of snakes is first revealed in *Raiders of the Lost Ark*, when Indiana discovers there is a snake aboard his rescue plane, and again later when he falls into a pit of snakes.
15. **True.** In the movie, a Lego character named Emmet must stop Lord Business from gluing the world together.
16. **False.** Percy must find the Golden Fleece in the sequel. In the original movie, *Percy Jackson & the Olympians: The Lightning Thief*, Percy is accused of stealing Zeus's lightning bolt.
17. **True.** Gru goes undercover in a bakery in order to learn who has stolen a secret Arctic laboratory.
18. **False.** Roar Omega Roar is a popular fraternity, while Oozma Kappa consists of misfits.
19. **False.** Superman battles General Zod in *Man of Steel*.
20. **False.** The story is about a Hobbit named Bilbo Baggins.

21. **True.** The half-animal, half-food creatures are created by Flint Lockwood's machine.
22. **True.** The setting of the movie was inspired by *The Mysterious Island* by Jules Verne, which was a sequel to his novel *Journey to the Center of the Earth*.
23. **False.** Haymitch Abernathy also won the Hunger Games as a District 12 resident.
24. **True.** Wolverine is summoned to Tokyo at the request of a dying man named Yashida, whom he encountered in a prison camp years earlier.
25. **True.** Elsa loses control of these powers and accidentally plunges the kingdom of Arendelle into winter.
26. **True.** Ender leads Dragon Army—a force that has never won a battle.
27. **True.** Mr. Peabody is an overachieving dog and Sherman is his adopted pet boy.
28. **True.** In the movie, it is revealed that Fiona's parents were about to make a deal with Rumpelstiltskin to be king in exchange for lifting Fiona's curse. But Shrek rescues Fiona before the deal is completed.
29. **False.** Nick Fury is the director of S.H.I.E.L.D., while Dr. Bruce Banner is a scientist who transforms into the Hulk.
30. **False.** Theodora turns into a green witch after biting into an apple given to her by Evanora.

All in the Family, pages 60–61

1. **a**   2. **d**
3. **False.** The five members of the Wanted met when they auditioned to be in the band.
4. **c**   5. **a**   6. **b**   7. **a**   8. **a**
9. **b**   10. **b**
11. **False.** The characters are both portrayed by one actress, Dove Cameron.
12. **b**   13. **b**

Game Central, pages 62–63

1. **b**   2. **d**   3. **a**   4. **b**   5. **a**
6. **b**   7. **c**   8. **d**   9. **a**   10. **a**
11. **c**   12. **d**   13. **a**   14. **c**

Game Show: Ultimate Pop Culture Challenge, pages 64–65

1. **c**   2. **c**   3. **a**
4. **False.** Dorothy's slippers are silver in the book. MGM executives decided to make the slippers ruby in the film, most likely because red looked better against the yellow brick road.
5. **b**
6. **a and h; b and e; c and g; d and f**
7. **d**
8. **b**
9. **b**
10. **a**
11. **a**
12. **c**
13. **a and h; b and e; c and f; d and g**
14. **b**

SCORING

0–32

BE YOURSELF!
You like reading about famous people and celebrities, TV shows, movies, and pop music. Yet you're someone who can balance being part of the in-crowd with independence and doing your own thing. Expanding your knowledge with this book will help you do that.

33–65

KEEP IT IN CHECK!
You've got your favorite TV shows and video games, but you know not to spend too much time on them. You don't want to be a couch potato. Using your leisure time wisely keeps you smart, healthy, and happy.

66–97

GO FOR GOLD!
You're top of the class, an ace at trivia, and a potential champion at *Quiz Whiz*! But there are always new things to learn, new challenges, and real-life adventures to be had, so don't stop now.

Natural WONDERS

Great Barrier Reef, pages 68–69

1. **False.** Coral is alive and made up of many small, soft-bodied creatures called polyps.
2. d
3. **True.** From space, the Great Barrier Reef looks like a light blue line off the coast of Australia.
4. c   5. a   6. d   7. b
8. b   9. d   10. a   11. c
12. **True.** The cuttlefish is a mollusk related to the octopus.

Forces of Nature, pages 70–71

1. a   2. c   3. b   4. a
5. **True.** A sinkhole in China in 2013 caused four buildings to collapse into the ground. Thankfully, no one was hurt.
6. a   7. b   8. b   9. d
10. **False.** The truck can go 120 miles an hour (193 km/h), but an avalanche can reach speeds of 200 miles an hour (322 km/h).
11. c
12. **False.** Scientists know that certain locations will have an earthquake sometime in the future, but they can't predict an exact date.
13. c   14. b   15. a

Life in Extremes, pages 72–73

1. b   2. c   3. a   4. b
5. **True.** Different types of bacteria living in and around the hot spring are colored yellow, green, orange, red, and brown.
6. d
7. **True.** During freezing-cold winters, snow is often the camels' only source of water, but they can only eat small amounts at a time.
8. a
9. **True.** A rock found in an animal's stomach is called a gastrolith.
10. a
11. **False.** However, scientists do suspect that Enceladus contains liquid water, one of the basic ingredients of life.
12. c

Starry Skies, pages 74–75

1. d   2. b
3. **False.** The stars only seem to line up when viewed from Earth. Actually, the stars of almost all constellations are in very different locations in space.
4. a   5. a   6. b   7. c   8. c
9. a   10. d   11. a   12. d
13. **False.** Stars move through space, but because they are so far away, they seem fixed in place. In 50,000 years, some constellations will look different.
14. **False.** Zodiac signs are constellations that fall on a band that seems to move around Earth as it rotates on its axis. Over the centuries, the timing has changed so that the traditional calendar of the Zodiac is not accurate anymore.
15. b

Nature in the Big City, pages 76–77

1. a   2. c
3. **True.** A cockroach's brain functions are spread around its body.
4. d
5. **False.** The Eiffel Tower gets about 7 million visits a year, and the Grand Canyon gets about 4 million.
6. **False.** Alligators are native to Florida, and couldn't survive for very long in cold, disease-ridden sewer water.
7. b   8. d   9. c   10. b
11. **True.** Clear glass windows kill the most birds, followed by house cats, electrical wires, then cars.
12. a
13. **True.** Leaves give off water vapor, cooling the air around them.
14. a   15. d

Map Mania! Famous Parks, pages 78–79

1. c   2. a   3. c   4. b
5. d   6. a   7. d   8. b
9. f   10. e   11. a   12. c

True or False? Into the Woods, pages 80–81

1. **True.** The oldest known bristlecone pine tree lived for about 4,900 years.
2. **False.** Just one in four hikers actually completes the journey.
3. **True.** The extreme heat of a forest fire makes jack pine cones open up.
4. **True.** An acre of grassland may contain more than 1 million spiders!
5. **False.** Hibernating black bears can go for 100 days without eating or drinking.
6. **False.** The banana slug is plenty big, though, at 6 to 10 inches (15 to 25 cm) long!
7. **True.** Big Ben is about 315 feet (96 m) tall, and Hyperion, the tallest redwood tree, stands at 379.1 feet (115.5 m).
8. **False.** As the weather gets colder in the fall, leaves stop producing chlorophyll, the chemical that keeps leaves green.
9. **True.** The boreal forest circles Earth, taking up much of northern Russia and Canada.
10. **True.** Predators might smell the chicks in the nest if they stay there for too long.
11. **True.** The trunk is 36.5 feet (11.1 m) wide and weighs nearly 1,400 tons (1,270 mT).
12. **True.** Flying snakes live in the jungles of Southeast Asia and can glide 330 feet (101 m).
13. **False.** Chicken-of-the-Woods is an edible mushroom.
14. **False.** A tree with about 50,000 leaves produces enough oxygen every hour for about five adults to breathe normally.
15. **True.** Crushed Moringa seeds can clean 99 percent of the bacteria out of water.
16. **False.** Flat oak leaves have a larger surface area than thin pine needles, so they capture more sunlight.
17. **True.** Pine sap is one defense trees have against beetle infestations.
18. **True.** The *Plethodontid* family of lungless salamanders must keep their skin moist in order to breathe.
19. **False.** White-tailed deer actually like to eat poison ivy!
20. **True.** The Black Forest is a popular vacation destination for hiking and mountain tours.
21. **True.** Native Americans were likely collecting and boiling down maple sap to make sugar as early as 1557.
22. **False.** Dendrochronologists study tree rings to learn about the condition of the environment in the past.
23. **True.** Periodical cicadas emerge in huge numbers on a regular cycle of every 13 or 17 years.
24. **True.** Deer shed their antlers in the spring, and a new set grows in 3 to 4 months.
25. **False.** Fiddleheads are edible baby ferns.
26. **False.** Diamond is the hardest mineral, and petrified wood is made up mainly of quartz.
27. **False.** Redwood trees have needles, not broad leaves.
28. **True.** Scientists showed that trees can take in tiny particles of gold from the soil.
29. **True.** The new mammals include a night monkey, porcupine, shrew, and four rodents.
30. **True.** Trees absorb carbon dioxide, the gas that causes global warming.

Game Show: Ultimate Nature Challenge, pages 82–83

1. b   2. a   3. b   4. b   5. a
6. c   7. d

8. **False.** Winters in the Gobi region are quite severe; temperatures can drop to -40°F (-40°C)

9. **d**   10. **b**   11. **c**   12. **c**   13. **b**

14. **True.** Fluorescence is common in the deep ocean, where light from the sun doesn't reach.

15. **a.** The white line is called the KT boundary, and it contains dust from the asteroid's impact.

SCORING

0–40
CITY SLICKER
You know your city block frontward, backward, and inside out, but the only flowers and trees you see each day live in little fenced-in holes in the sidewalk. Take a trip to the mountains or the ocean and bask in nature's glory!

41–80
COUNTRY-WISE
Out on the farm, you've got lots of time to dig soil, feed livestock, gaze at the stars, and ask questions. You're on the way to an exciting future exploring the outdoors, and maybe birdwatching, making cheese, and planting your own garden.

81–126
RAISED BY WOLVES
The only way you could possibly know so much is if you were raised out in the woods! Seriously, you've got the natural instincts of a wolf, you're as wise as an owl, and you have the book smarts of a super nature genius. You're certainly top dog at this game.

Back in TIME

Fashion Fads, pages 86–87
1. **c**   2. **c**   3. **a**   4. **a**
5. **True.** It goes back to "Charles the Bald" in the eighth century.
6. **False.** Crocs are foam shoes with vent holes in them; the fur-lined boots are called UGGs.
7. **b**
8. **b**
9. **c**
10. **True.** It was known as "space-age fashion."
11. **b**
12. **b**
13. **c**

Famous Pets, pages 88–89
1. **b**   2. **a**   3. **d**
4. **False.** She grew up on a farm, probably taking care of cattle and sheep.
5. **c**   6. **b**   7. **c**   8. **b**
9. **c.** After Meredith Grey in *Grey's Anatomy*.
10. **True.** She also owned Mrs. Tiggy-Winkle the hedgehog, Spot the spaniel, Xarifa the mouse, and Pig-Wig the pig.
11. **False.** But he did write a song about his pet sheepdog, Martha.

Toy Story, pages 90–91
1. **c**   2. **a**   3. **b**   4. **c**
5. **b**   6. **b**
7. **False.** That is when mass production of marbles began, but they had been around for thousands of years.
8. **a**   9. **c**   10. **c**
11. **a**
12. **b**
13. **False.** The Game Boy video game was released in February, with the cards following in October.

Blast From the Past: Pompeii, pages 92–93
1. **c**   2. **c**   3. **b**   4. **a**   5. **b**
6. **False.** We know what happened because a man interviewed the survivors and recorded the events in a letter.
7. **b**
8. **True.** Pompeii art and reproductions of ruins were popular decorations.
9. **a**   10. **c**
11. **False.** It last erupted on March 18, 1944. Scientists believe it could erupt again soon.
12. **True**   13. **b**   14. **c**

Let the Games Begin, pages 94–95
1. **c**   2. **b**   3. **a**   4. **c**
5. **True.** Other English games with similarities to baseball include cricket and rounders.
6. **b**   7. **c**   8. **d**
9. **False.** In 1905, colleges decided to allow the forward pass. (The touchdown was not worth six points until 1912.)
10. **c**   11. **a**   12. **c**   13. **True**

ANSWERS

True or False?
Read All About It!,
pages 96–97

1. **True.** Gilgamesh was an actual king about the year 2700 B.C. It is unlikely he searched for eternal life, though!
2. **False.** There are roosters in *Aesop's Fables*, but no monkeys.
3. **True.** The collection also brought us Ali Baba and Sinbad the Sailor.
4. **False.** The Sagas were written in Iceland in the 1200s and 1300s.
5. **True.** The British expression "tilting at windmills" comes from this scene.
6. **False.** Earth is not named after a god!
7. **True.** Leslie shared them with Jess, and also shared *Hamlet, Moby-Dick*, and the Chronicles of Prydain series.
8. **False.** Thor, the god of thunder, is considered the guardian of the gods. But Odin is the king.
9. **True.** Gutenberg tested his invention by printing a book about speechmaking in 1450. He then moved on to printing Bibles, which he became famous for.
10. **True.** No woman legally appeared on an English stage until 1660.
11. **False.** There have been two movie versions: *Willy Wonka & the Chocolate Factory* (1971) and *Charlie and the Chocolate Factory* (2005).
12. **False.** *Robinson Crusoe* is an early English novel, but not the first. There are several books this claim has been made about.
13. **False.** They were about 6 inches (15 cm) tall.
14. **True.** She is trying to save Wilbur the pig.
15. **False.** The monster did not have a name. Its creator's name was Victor Frankenstein.
16. **False.** *The Glasgow Looking Glass*, published in Scotland in 1825, is now considered to be the first comic book. *Obadiah Oldbuck* is believed to be the first comic book published in the U.S.A.
17. **True.** His book *Twenty Years After*, from 1845, is a sequel to *The Three Musketeers*.
18. **True.** It is said that Stevenson then rewrote the 30,000 words by hand in three days.
19. **True.** The TV series, *Little House on the Prairie*, ran until 1983.
20. **False.** There are no records of Tolkien writing any plays.
21. **True.** He was in the French Air Force and also delivered airmail in Africa.
22. **False.** He was Clive Staples Lewis.
23. **True.** Project Gutenberg still exists, with more than 44,000 e-books that people can download for free.
24. **False.** The first Mary Poppins book came out in 1934.
25. **True.** The series has sold more than 450 million books worldwide.
26. **False.** There is no such network. However, on weekends, the network C-SPAN2 becomes "Book TV," with shows about nonfiction books.
27. **True.** As a crow she would often fly over the battlefield.
28. **True.** In 1779, a man named Hans Fuchs claimed he saw *two* of this imaginary creature.
29. **False.** She originally titled it *Forks*, but her agent suggested they choose another name.
30. **True.** It took more than 50 people to make the book, titled *This the Prophet Mohammed*.

Lost Worlds,
pages 98–99

1. **True.** At the 25-acre site called Göbekli Tepe, there are 7 (or more) stone circles.
2. b   3. c   4. a   5. c
6. **True.** Satellite images started revealing the shapes in 1999.
7. a   8. b   9. c   10. c   11. c
12. **False.** We made this one up.
13. a

Party Time!,
pages 100–101

1. a   2. c
3. **True.** It is an important event in the Hindu religion, taking place where three rivers meet—the Ganga, Yamuna, and Saraswati.
4. c   5. c   6. b   7. b   8. a
9. **False.** The people throw oranges at these masked characters called "Gilles" at the annual Carnival of Binche.
10. b
11. **True.**

Map Mania!
Rotten Rulers,
pages 102–103

1. a   2. b   3. a   4. c   5. b
6. c   7. 1D   8. 2A   9. 3C   10. 4F
11. 5E   12. 6B

Game Show: Ultimate
Time Travel Challenge,
pages 104–105

1. b   2. c   3. a   4. b
5. **True.** A handheld cutting device called a scythe was also used.
6. b   7. a   8. c
9. **False.** But today, some people will do this when walking on icy ground!
10. c   11. b   12. c
13. **True.** Washington Irving published them in 1819 to 1820.
14. b   15. b

SCORING

0–49

HERE AND NOW
You're into the present day, but you can learn more about the past by starting with your own family. Ask your parents, aunts, and uncles where your family came from. Check if any of them have documents that will help you find out the history.

50–98

MOVING FORWARD
It's a well-held belief that history repeats itself. And fashions come and go...and come again. Therefore, knowledge of the past and following trends will help you shape ideas and plans both for the present day and the future.

99–145

FUTURE LEADER
With such a high score, it is clear you are a history maven. Build on your knowledge of the past to shape the future. Follow your passions and dreams and set your path into the history books. You are master of your own destiny.

We've Got Your NUMBER

Color by Numbers, pages 108–109

1. b   2. b   3. c   4. c
5. **False.** About 1 in every 200 has red hair.
6. c   7. a   8. c   9. b
10. **True.** They are also very good swimmers.
11. **False.** Dogs can see shades of yellow, blue, and gray.
12. a   13. b

Mount Rushmore Math, pages 110–111

1. c   2. b   3. c   4. c   5. a
6. b
7. **True.** The faces are each 60 feet (18.3 m) high.
8. a   9. b
10. **False.** The project was started by sculptor Korczak Ziolkowski in 1948, and his family still continues to work on it.
11. b   12. c   13. b   14. c   15. b

What's Cooking?, pages 112–113

1. b   2. a   3. c   4. c   5. b
6. **True.** The word "burrito" first appears in a Mexican book from 1898.
7. **False.** It's 250 to 300 eggs per year.
8. b   9. b   10. a   11. c   12. b
13. c

True or False? It's About Time, pages 114–115

1. **True.** On that day, Germany invaded Poland.
2. **False.** A cheetah can run 70 miles an hour (112.7 km/h).
3. **True.** The idea was called Y2K, with the fear that computers would think 2000 was really 1900.
4. **True.** Adding one penny to the mechanism causes the clock to speed up by two-fifths of a second over 24 hours.
5. **False.** It was that day and time, but in 1969, not 1970.
6. **True.** The white-throated needletail is the fastest bird in normal flight, supposedly reaching 105 miles an hour (169 km/h).
7. **False.** He landed in the Bahamas.
8. **True.** The peace agreement between Germany and the Allied Forces was signed just after 5 a.m., but it went into effect at 11 a.m.
9. **True.** It is to keep our time similar to the planet's rotation.
10. **False.** The sailfish can reach 68 miles an hour (109.4 km/h).
11. **False.** The document was adopted by Congress on July 4, 1776, but signed on August 2, 1776.
12. **True.** Britain had controlled Hong Kong since 1842, except for brief rule by Japan during World War II.
13. **False.** The Wall was put up on that day. It stood until November 9, 1989, when people finally tore it down.
14. **False.** Bannister was the first to run the mile in under 4 minutes. The current record is 3 minutes, 43.13 seconds, set by Hicham El Guerrouj of Morocco in 1999.
15. **True.** The system was meant to keep factories running all the time. In 1931, they changed to 6-day weeks, finally returning to 7-day weeks in 1940.
16. **False.** It sank on April 15, with the loss of more than 1,500 passengers and crew.
17. **False.** Fourteen days is known as a "fortnight."
18. **False.** It was March 10, 1876.
19. **True.** Mats Valk of the Netherlands did it in March 2013.
20. **True.** Track superstar Usain Bolt achieved a speed of 27.79 miles an hour (44.72 km/h), while a red kangaroo can reach 35 miles an hour (56.3 km/h).
21. **False.** Since 1675—by international agreement—each day, year, and millennium begins at the Royal Observatory in London, England.
22. **False.** Su Song built an impressive clock run by water, but the sun and water had both been used for clocks for thousands of years before that.
23. **True.** The average litter is six pups, but most don't make it to adulthood.
24. **True.** They fall very slowly—in all those years, only 8 drops (and possibly a 9th, recently) have fallen.
25. **True.** The North Berwick, Maine, man set the record in 2010 with 1,509 working clocks.
26. **False.** It is from Latin, *minutus*, meaning "small."
27. **False.** Yeager went faster than the speed of sound, not light (that is much, much faster).
28. **True.** It is called Nepal Standard Time.
29. **True.** They use a 12-month calendar. However, on their "Juche" calendar, the years began with 1912, the birth of their first leader, Kim Il-Sung. So 2012 was "Juche 101."
30. **True.** Slower than this and the spacecraft falls back to Earth or into orbit around the planet.

Money Matters, pages 116–117

1. c   2. b   3. c   4. b   5. c
6. **True.** In 1748, a man named Conrad Weiser wrote in his journal, "He has been robbed of the value of 300 Bucks."
7. b
8. **True.** There is a picture of a common loon on the back, a bird that is often seen in Canada.
9. b   10. a   11. b
12. **False.** A stack of 1 trillion bills would be 67,000 miles (107,826 km) long, which is about 2.7 times around Earth's circumference.

Map Mania! Supersized Structures, pages 118–119

1. b   2. c   3. a
4. c   5. d   6. a
7. 1D   8. 2E   9. 3B
10. 4C   11. 5F   12. 6A

Game Show: Ultimate Giant Challenge, pages 120–121

1. b   2. c   3. c   4. a   5. c
6. **True.** There were seven different buildings, with the Empire State Building holding the title from 1931 to 1970.
7. c   8. b   9. b
10. **False.** Nickels are 25 percent nickel, and the rest is "cupronickel"—copper blended with some nickel.
11. **False.** Washington was the 1st president and Jefferson was the 3rd, but Lincoln was the 16th and Roosevelt was the 26th.
12. c   13. a   14. b
15. **b.** In a poll of car buyers, the results were: blue 9 percent, red 10 percent, yellow 2 percent, green 3 percent.

SCORING

0–37

NUMBER NOVICE
If math is a mystery and number-crunching makes your brain fizz, don't worry. Keep on counting and you'll get there! Focus on what you do best. Every new fact and figure you learn adds to your knowledge.

38–74

IT ALL ADDS UP
So you don't need a calculator to tally your score, but you're not a number wizard just yet. Your brain loves numbers but it wants to learn more. Keep counting!

75–110

NUMBER ONE
You're clearly at home with numbers, and your family and friends can count on you in trivia quizzes. You could grow up to be a mathematical genius.

Amazing SCIENCE

Dinosaur Days, pages 124–125

1. **b**   2. **c**
3. **False.** Birds evolved about 150 million years ago, some 80 million years before dinosaurs died out.
4. **False.** *Tyrannosaurus rex*'s bite was about twice as powerful as that of a great white shark.
5. **a**   6. **c**
7. **False.** *Alamosaurus* was about 69 feet (21 m) long, almost 3 times the size of an elephant.
8. **c**
9. **True.** The dinosaur's scary head inspired paleontologists to name it for the fictional character.
10. **b**   11. **b**   12. **d**   13. **b**   14. **d**
15. **True.** Feathered birds evolved from feathered dinosaurs.

The Dirt on Dirt, pages 126–127

1. **c**
2. **False.** Only one out of every billion atoms in Earth's crust is gold.
3. **True.** Mud keeps the elephants' skin moist and kills parasites.
4. **b**   5. **c**   6. **a**   7. **c**   8. **d**
9. **b**   10. **b**   11. **d**   12. **b**   13. **b**
14. **True.** Many pumice rocks float in water.
15. **True.** Mud volcanoes on Mars are mounds that likely bring up wet material from below the surface.

Gross Out, pages 128–129

1. **b**   2. **c**
3. **True.** We each have our own body odor.
4. **b**   5. **d**   6. **a**   7. **d**   8. **d**
9. **True.** Normally, your body keeps the fungus population low.
10. **d**   11. **b**
12. **False.** Kangaroos (and cows, people, and many other animals) all fart to release intestinal gas.

Eco-Challenge, pages 130–131

1. **c**   2. **b**
3. **False.** Some deep-sea fish get energy from hot undersea vents rather than the sun.

4. **a**   5. **b**   6. **d**   7. **c**
8. **True.** Baby fawns are born in the spring, causing the deer population to increase.
9. **d**   10. **b**   11. **b**
12. **False.** It's not easy, but ships called skimmers and some types of bacteria can clean up spilled oil.
13. **b**   14. **a**

True or False? Shape Up, pages 132–133

1. **False.** Experts can even spin a Hula-Hoop on one foot while doing a handstand!
2. **False.** A 9-year-old girl or boy has to do 18 push-ups to qualify for the award.
3. **True.** The distance is exactly 90 feet (27 m) between each base.
4. **False.** Scrambled eggs have about twice as much saturated fat as pizza.
5. **True.** Jumping and dressage are two Olympic sports where horses compete (along with their human riders, of course).
6. **False.** Yoga is a form of exercise that involves stretching and holding different body positions.
7. **True.** The chemicals are called endorphins. They also reduce stress and pain.
8. **True.** Alan Shepard hit two golf balls on the moon in 1971. The balls are still up there!
9. **False.** A study showed that women who slept 5 hours or less per night were 30 percent more likely to gain weight.
10. **False.** As of 2011, Ivo Karlovic of Croatia held the record for the fastest serve at 156 miles an hour (251 km/h).
11. **True.** Zumba comes from Colombia, South America.
12. **False.** Your brain likely cleans out toxins while you sleep, and it also produces dreams.
13. **True.** The most popular form of exercise is walking.

14. **False.** A healthy diet includes daily servings of fruits and vegetables.
15. **False.** As of 2013, the record for the fastest marathon is 2 hours and 3 minutes.
16. **False.** Twelve-year-old pitchers can throw faster than chimps!
17. **False.** Babies have more than 300 bones, while adults have 206.
18. **True.** If you drink one can of soda every day for a year, you could gain as much as 5 pounds (2.2 kg).
19. **True.** Broccoli, spinach, and tomatoes also contain high amounts of vitamin C.
20. **True.** Exercise can also lower the risk of some cancers, diabetes, and bone problems.
21. **False.** Judo is similar to wrestling and originated in Japan.
22. **False.** Your body burns calories to keep your organs, muscles, and brain going.
23. **False.** Vegans don't eat any animal products, and eggs come from chickens.
24. **True.** The more time people spend sitting, the fewer years they are expected to live.
25. **True.** People also bike longer and swim faster while listening to music.

26. **False.** Fat and muscles are two very different parts of your body.
27. **False.** Raw vegetables tend to have more vitamin C, but cooked vegetables provide other nutrients that are important to your health.
28. **True.** The sport debuted at the 1988 Summer Olympics in Seoul, South Korea.
29. **False.** A treadmill helps you practice running or jogging.
30. **True.** Only about 16 percent of people play a sport or exercise on any given day.

Tech Trek, pages 134–135
1. b
2. **True.** Electronic computers and calculators eventually replaced human computers.
3. d   4. c   5. a   6. b   7. b
8. **False.** Today's cell phones (and most pocket calculators, modern cars, and USB drives) have more processing power than the Apollo 11 computers did.
9. a   10. b
11. **True.** MANIAC stood for Mathematical Analyzer, Numerical Integrator, And Computer.
12. c   13. c   14. d   15. c

Mad Scientists, pages 136–137
1. d   2. c   3. a   4. b
5. d   6. c   7. c   8. a
9. a   10. c   11. b   12. b

Animal Name Game, pages 138–139
1. c   2. b   3. d
4. **True.** If you ever come upon a quiver of poisonous king cobras, run away!
5. a   6. c   7. c   8. c
9. c   10. a   11. a
12. **False.** The bat looks like it has suction cups on its feet, but actually holds on with a sticky liquid.
13. b

Game Show: Ultimate Science Challenge, pages 140–141
1. b
2. **False.** An adult has 26 foot bones, and 180 bones in the rest of the body.
3. d   4. a
5. **True.** One tiny solar-powered computer helps patients with an eye disease keep track of their eyes' health.
6. b   7. b   8. d   9. a
10. **True.** The photo is of a female—these cones grow much larger than males and contain seeds.
11. d
12. a
13. **False.** Skunk spray isn't dangerous, but it sure is stinky! Most predators leave skunks alone.
14. c
15. c

SCORING

0–47

COUNTDOWN
You're not out of this world just yet, but your interest in science is about to take off. Visit a local science museum, surf the Internet, and watch some science documentaries to help you on your voyage of exploration and discovery.

48–94

SPARKS ARE FLYING
You're a bright spark and live wire, so get inventing. Challenge yourself, work out a line of investigation, experiment, examine your results, and draw your conclusions. We hope your inventions are worth the effort!

95–141

EUREKA!
So exclaimed a scientist as he leaped out of the bath having solved a watery problem. Science is your thing. May you have lots of eureka moments as you try to become the next great scientific genius.

Awesome ADVENTURES

Climbing Mount Everest, pages 144–145

1. b   2. c   3. a   4. c   5. d
6. b   7. b   8. d   9. c
10. **True.** After hearing stories about a yeti in the Himalaya, Hillary and a group of people searched the region's Rowaling Valley for clues but found no evidence to confirm the creature's existence.
11. a   12. a   13. b

Galaxy Quest, pages 146–147

1. c
2. **False.** The Apollo astronauts claimed that moondust smelled like gunpowder.
3. b   4. b   5. b
6. **True.** The lifelike dummy was used to test the safety of the spacecraft and suit before cosmonaut Yuri Gagarin became the first human in space.
7. b   8. a
9. **False.** It was named after two different ships sailed by famous explorers, Henry Hudson and James Cook.
10. a   11. c   12. d   13. a   14. c

Samurai Warriors, pages 148–149

1. b   2. d   3. b   4. c
5. c   6. a   7. a
8. **True.** Most female samurai did not fight in battles, but they did defend their homes if attacked.
9. b   10. d   11. c   12. c

True or False? Famous Explorations, pages 150–151

1. **True.** Conquistadors ("conquerors" in Spanish) took over areas such as present-day Mexico and Peru.
2. **False.** Roald Dahl, who authored many books including *Charlie and the Chocolate Factory*, was named after Roald Amundsen—the first known person to reach the South Pole.
3. **True.** Food supply ships carried large tubs of earth from which vegetables were grown.
4. **True.** Caver Gennady Samokhin descended 7,208 feet (2,197 m) down Krubera Cave in the sovereign state of Georgia. By comparison, the Empire State Building only measures 1,467 feet (447 m).
5. **True.** Club de Regatas Vasco da Gama is named after the Portuguese explorer.
6. **False.** Although Pocahontas may have helped Smith, she ultimately married John Rolfe.
7. **True.** A crewman aboard Hudson's ship claimed he saw a mermaid.
8. **True.** From 1990 to 1994, the Magellan spacecraft mapped and took photos of the surface of Venus.
9. **True.** Some historians believe that Erikson was heading to Greenland when he sailed off course and ended up in a part of Canada.
10. **False.** Charles Lindbergh was the first to achieve this feat. He flew from New York to Paris in 1927.
11. **False.** The Chinese are believed to have been the first people to use a compass for navigation in 1100.
12. **False.** Europe, Africa, and Asia were known as the "Old World," while North and South America were regarded as the "New World" after the voyages of European explorers.
13. **False.** Although many archeologists believed that the ancient Chinese first ate pasta, it is unlikely that Marco Polo introduced the food to Italy.
14. **True.** During 1913 and 1914, Roosevelt, along with Brazilian explorer Candido Rondon, was part of an expedition to map the then uncharted Amazon River.
15. **False.** Matthew A. Henson and Robert E. Peary traveled together to the North Pole. Lewis and Clark traveled across the American Midwest to the Pacific Ocean.
16. **True.** Although some people celebrated the 300th anniversary of Columbus's arrival in the Americas in 1792, it did not become an official holiday for another hundred years.
17. **True.** After Ponce de León's death in 1521, numerous accounts emerged of a possible quest to find a mythical fountain of youth.
18. **False.** Earle learned to swim in her family pool in New Jersey and has spent much of her career in the water.
19. **True.** To determine the direction of land on a foggy day, Vikings would release a crow from their ship and then follow the direction in which it flew.
20. **False.** The shipwreck was discovered by deep-sea explorer Robert Ballard. However Cameron, who developed the movie *Titanic*, has explored the wreck.
21. **False.** The submersible was named after Allyn Vine, a pioneer of deep-sea exploration.
22. **True.** The Giant Crystal Cave is filled with crystals that measure up to 36 feet (11 m) long.
23. **True.** It took them 94 days to complete the 1,717-mile (2,763-km) trek.
24. **True.** It took Fossett 14 days and 9 hours to circle the globe.
25. **True.** Many sailors contracted scurvy, which results from a lack of vitamin C, which is found in many fruits and vegetables.
26. **True.** Sir Francis Drake plundered many Spanish ports and had a terrible reputation with the Spanish.
27. **False.** Columbus and his crew discovered hammocks in the Bahamas, where the Taino people used them.
28. **False.** Susan B. Anthony and Helen Keller have appeared on U.S. coins in circulation.
29. **True.** Marco Polo's expedition began in 1271 when he was 17 years old and ended in 1295.
30. **True.** *Santa Clara* was the ship's official name. Columbus and his crew often called the ship by its nickname—*Niña*—after the ship's owner, Juan Niño.

Camp Thrills, pages 152–153

1. c   2. a   3. c   4. d
5. **True.** Mosquitoes are attracted to heat and carbon dioxide. Since adults are larger than kids, they emit more heat and carbon dioxide, and therefore tend to attract more mosquitoes.
6. b   7. d   8. d
9. **True.** At the Zombie Summer Camp in Burlington, Massachusetts, campers use Nerf Blasters to fight off actors dressed as zombies.
10. b   11. d   12. b   13. a   14. c

Map Mania! Dig It Up!, pages 154–155

1. **True.** Naturalist Robert Plot initially thought the bone may have belonged to an ancient Roman elephant, but then concluded that it must have come from a giant human.
2. b   3. d   4. a   5. b   6. b
7. d   8. a   9. 1B   10. 2C   11. 3D
12. 4H   13. 5G   14. 6A   15. 7E   16. 8F

Game Show: Ultimate Adventure Challenge, pages 156–57

1. b
2. **True.** The roller coaster reaches a height of 415 feet (126 m), while the Statue of Liberty measures 305.6 feet (93 m).
3. **False.** Horned helmets may have been worn by northern Europeans long before the Vikings, but scientists have never uncovered a Viking helmet with horns.
4. c   5. d   6. d   7. b   8. b
9. **True.** Although Mount Everest is the world's highest mountain at 29,035 feet (8,848 m), it is not the tallest. Mauna Kea in Hawaii rises 33,476 feet (10,203 m) from the ocean floor, making it the tallest mountain on Earth.
10. c   11. c   12. c   13. b   14. d

169

SCORING

0–38
SLOW STARTER
You're not the first one out the door when invited to come out and play, but we can't all be movers and shakers. You're just starting on the quest for knowledge but are eager to pick up new facts and figures.

39–76
UP FOR ACTION
You've got a taste for exploration and are ready for new challenges. That's a surefire combination for success. If you experience a setback, you'll get back on your feet, dust yourself down, and be back in action in no time.

77–113
FAST MOVER
Quick off the mark and racing ahead, you're ready for adventure. Your knowledge and sense of adventure will take you far, but don't be reckless. Remember to stay safe and to stay on the right track. You may not climb every mountain but you could conquer the world.

GRAND TALLY

Are you a *Quiz Whiz* champion? Do you deserve a gold star? How have you done on our quiz? Do you consider yourself an ace at animals, a genius of geography, and magical at math? Tally your scores from all eight chapters to learn how you stack up against other brainiacs. Use the chart below to find out your *Quiz Whiz* status.

0–345
TRIVIA NOVICE
With this score, you are on a learning curve and have a good way to go, but you have the desire to improve, so run with that. Try a variety of quizzes and puzzles and test your knowledge whenever you can. Read lots of books, magazines, and newspapers and keep asking questions to get those brain cells working. Your brain is like a sponge so feed it with facts, figures, and trivia. Much of this will soak in and take you to the next level.

346–690
APPRENTICE
You're halfway to becoming a quizmeister but you need to build up your knowledge and experience of unfamiliar subjects. Take on new challenges and set new goals. There's lots more to learn!

691–1,029
THE WHIZ OF QUIZ
Congratulations on a terrific score. You're in a *Quiz Whiz* league of your own. What you have is clearly not artificial intelligence but a well-trained brain, a desire to learn, and a quest for knowledge.

41 [UP], Nilanjan Bhattacharya/DRMS; 41 [CTR], Richard Griffin/DRMS; 41 [LO], Szefei/
DRMS; 44 [UP], Sergey Denisov/DRMS; 44 [CTR], Kingjon/DRMS; 44 [LO], Sahua/DRMS; 45
[UP], Sikth/DRMS; 45 [CTR], Ron Chapple/DRMS; 45 [LO], Alecrain/DRMS; 46-47 [BKGD],
Hurst Photo/SS; 48 [1], Surabky/DRMS; 48 [2], Brad Calkins/DRMS; 48 [3], Leswag/DRMS;
48 [4], Péter Gudella/DRMS; 49 [5], Lukas Blazek/DRMS; 49 [6], Johnjewell/DRMS; 49
[7], Mazuciukas/DRMS; 50 [UP], Editor77/DRMS; 50 [CTR], Chrispethick/DRMS; 50 [LO],
Cheri131/DRMS; 51 [UP], Iakov Filimonov/DRMS; 51 [CTR], José Marafona/DRMS; 51 [LO-
A], Michael Flippo/DRMS; 51 [LO-B], Christoph Weihs/DRMS; 51 [LO-C], Andreblais/DRMS;
51 [LO-D], Vladescu Bogdan/DRMS

Pop Culture [52-65]
52-53, [BKGD], United Archives/TF; 54 [UP], Featureflash/SS; 54 [CTR], Damedeeso/DRMS;
54 [LO], Sbukley/DRMS; 55 [CTR], United Archives/TF; 55 [LO], Jstone/SS; 57 [BKGD], 2006/
TF; 60 [UP], Imago/Actionplus/TF; 60 [CTR], Thomas Dutour/DRMS; 61 [UP], Lee6713/
DRMS; 61 [LO], Michael Flippo/DRMS; 62-63, Beaniebeagle/DRMS; 64 [UP], Yianniskourt/
DRMS; 64 [CTR], Mvogel/DRMS; 64 [LO], Isselee/DRMS; 65 [UP LE], Carrienelson1/DRMS;
65 [UP RT], Sahua/DRMS; 65 [LO-A], Carrienelson1/DRMS; 65 [LO-B], Featureflash/DRMS;
65 [LO-C], Jason957/DRMS; 65 [LO-D], Yakub88/DRMS

Natural Wonders [66-83]
66-67 [BKGD], Vilainecrevette/DRMS; 68 [UP], Tolly81/DRMS; 68 [CTR], paul cowell/SS; 68
[LO], Stephankerkhofs/DRMS; 69 [UP], Kasia Biel/DRMS; 69 [CTR], Ruslan Gilmanshin/
DRMS; 69 [LO], Melvinlee/DRMS; 70-71 [BKGD], Leighdiprosephotography/DRMS; 72 [UP],
Ultrashock/SS; 72 [CTR], Courtesy NASA/JPL-Caltech/NASA; 72 [LO], Lorcel G/DRMS;
73 [UP], Afonskaya Irina/DRMS; 73 [LO], Anankkml/DRMS; 74-75 [BKGD], Natthawut
Punyosaeng/DRMS; 76-77 [BKGD], Songquan Deng/DRMS; 78 [1], Jankojerinic/DRMS;
78 [2], Dmitry Pichugin/DRMS; 78 [3], Nico Smit/DRMS; 79 [4], Lambert [bart] Parren/
DRMS; 79 [5], Christopher Boswell/SS; 79 [6], Martin Lehmann/DRMS; 82 [UP], Wangkun
Jia/DRMS; 82 [CTR], Santia2/DRMS; 82 [LO], Jakub Krechowicz/DRMS; 83 [UP], Erica
Schroeder/DRMS; 83 [CTR LE], Pierre-Yves Babelon/SS; 83 [CTR RT], Skafy1/DRMS; 83
[LO], Eurico Zimbres/www.en.wikipedia.org/wiki/File:K-T-boundary.JPG/WIKI

Back in Time [84-105]
84-85 [BKGD], Fine Art Images/Heritage Images/TF; 86 [UP], Land of Lost Content/HIP/TF;
86 [LO], MANDY GODBEHEAR/SS; 87 [UP], ©ullsteinbild/TF; 87 [LO], Dorling Kindersley/GI;
89 [LO], István Csák/DRMS; 90 [UP], The Granger Collection/TF; 90 [CTR LE], Gualtiero Boffi/
DRMS; 90 [CTR RT], Gsrethees/DRMS; 90 [LO], Omidii/DRMS; 91 [UP], Ivonne Wierink/DRMS;
91 [CTR], Elena Schweitzer/SS; 91 [LO], Constantin Opris/DRMS; 92-93 [BKGD], NGKids; 94
[UP], 2004/TF; 94 [LO], Daniela Pelazza/DRMS; 95 [UP], Georgii Dolgykh/DRMS; 95 [CTR LE],
Volkop/DRMS; 95 [CTR RT], Nicholas Piccillo/SS; 95 [LO], Imago/Actionplus/TF; 98 [UP], The

Granger Collection/TF; 98 [CTR], Kudinovart/DRMS; 98 [LO], World History Archive/TF; 99 [UP], Nialldunne24/DRMS; 99 [LO], AMC Photography/SS; 100-101 [BKGD], GuoZhongHua/SS; 102 [1], Heaton/TF; 102 [2], Roger-Viollet/TF; 102 [3], IgorGolovniov/SS; 103 [4], Peter Zachar/SS; 103 [5], Fine Art Images/Heritage Images/TF; 103 [6], 2000 Credit:Topham/AP/TF; 104 [UP], Bruce Jenkins/DRMS; 104 [LO LE], Olga Galkina/DRMS; 104 [LO RT], Isselee/DRMS; 105 [UP], Rafael Angel Irusta Machin/DRMS; 105 [CTR], Oreena/DRMS; 105 [LO-A], Eileen/DRMS; 105 [LO-B], Richard Thomas/DRMS; 105 [LO-C], Maximus117/DRMS; 105 [LO-D], Aliaksei Asipovich/DRMS

We've Got Your Number [106-121]
106-107 [BKGD], salajean/SS; 108 [UP], Jiri Hera/SS; 108 [CTR], 2004 ImageWorks/TF; 108 [LO LE], Pavel Svoboda/DRMS; 108 [LO RT], Iakov Filimonov/SS; 109 [UP], Chrishowey/DRMS; 109 [CTR], David Burke/DRMS; 109 [LO], Gunnar Assmy/SS; 110-111 [BKGD], Andreykr/DRMS; 112-113 [BKGD], Leonid Yastremskiy/DRMS; 116 [UP], Elnur/SS; 116 [LO LE], HamsterMan/SS; 116 [LO RT], Phase4Studios/SS; 117 [UP], Dave Bredeson/DRMS; 117 [CTR LE], Peter Spirer/DRMS; 117 [CTR RT], Sergey Sundikov/DRMS; 117 [LO], Seif1958/DRMS; 118 [1], Action Sports Photography/SS; 118 [2], Leonard Zhukovsky/SS; 118 [3], Richard Semik/DRMS; 119 [4], Andrew Cornaga/Actionplus/TF; 119 [5], PRILL/SS; 119 [6], Robert Gubiani/DRMS; 120 [UP], Michael Gray/DRMS; 120 [CTR], Checco/DRMS; 120 [LO LE], Speculator27/DRMS; 120 [LO RT], Robert Wisdom/DRMS; 121 [UP], Merzavka/DRMS; 121 [CTR LE], Drhuckstable/DRMS; 121 [CTR RT], rook76/SS; 121 [LO], Clippingpath1/DRMS

Amazing Science [122-141]
122-123 [BKGD], NGKids; 124-125 [BKGD], Computer Earth/SS; 126 127 [BKGD], fotoslaz/SS; 128 [UP], sherrie smith/DRMS; 128 [CTR], Aurora Photos/RH; 128 [LO], Alexander Raths/DRMS; 129 [UP], Nilsz/DRMS; 129 [CTR], Photographerlondon/DRMS; 129 [LO], Anankkml/DRMS; 130-131 [BKGD], Balazs Justin/SS; 134-135 [BKGD], Sayid/SS; 136 [UP], Yael Weiss/DRMS; 136 [CTR], TF; 136 [LO], 2005 TF; 137 [UP], Ronald Grant Archive/TF; 137 [LO], Ron Leishman/SS; 138 [UP], age fotostock/RH; 138 [CTR], Isselee/DRMS; 138 [LO], LauraD/SS; 139 [UP LE], Yinan Zhang/DRMS; 139 [UP RT], IFREMER/A.FIFIS/National Geographic Creative; 139 [CTR], KELLEY MILLER/National Geographic Creative; 139 [LO], Marina Jay/SS; 140 [UP], leonello calvetti/SS; 140 [CTR], Sebastian Kaulitzki/DRMS; 140 [LO], Ebgordon/DRMS; 141 [UP LE], Olavs Silis/DRMS; 141 [UP-A], Igor Stramyk/DRMS; 141 [UP-B], Ana Vasileva/DRMS; 141 [UP-C], Anankkml/DRMS; 141 [UP-D], Erik Lam/DRMS; 141 [LO LE], Isselee/DRMS; 141 [LO RT], Alisbalb/DRMS

Awesome Adventures [142-157]
142-143 [BKGD], Mikadun/SS; 144 [UP], PlusONE/SS; 144 [CTR], Zzvet/SS; 144 [LO], Cosmin-Constantin Sava/DRMS; 145 [UP], Kwiktor/DRMS; 145 [LO], Albert Ziganshin/

SS; 146-147 [BKGD], Kevin Key/SS; 148 [UP], The Granger Collection/TF; 148 [LO], ayelet-keshet/SS; 149 [UP], Avian/DRMS; 149 [CTR], Radu Razvan Gheorghe/DRMS; 149 [LO], Ken Backer/DRMS; 152-153 [BKGD], RHIMAGE/SS; 154 [1], Artmedia/Heritage Images/TF; 154 [2], Catmando/SS; 154 [3], Bob Orsillo/SS; 154 [4], Tyler Olson/SS; 155 [5], Linda Bucklin/SS; 155 [6], Ryan M. Bolton/SS; 155 [7], Michael Rosskothen/SS; 155 [8], Catmando/SS; 156 [UP], Aquariagirl1970/DRMS; 156 [CTR], Jean-Michel Girard/SS; 156 [LO], Ammit/DRMS; 157 [UP], Jeff Schultes/SS; 157 [CTR LE], Mike Heywood/DRMS; 157 [CTR RT], outdoorsman/SS; 157 [LO-A], Christopher Elwell/DRMS; 157 [LO-B], Saporob/DRMS; 157 [LO-C], Andersastphoto/DRMS; 157 [LO-D], Mircea Costina/DRMS

Answer Key [158-170]
158 [UP LE], Roger Calger/DRMS; 158 [UP RT], Mana Photo/SS; 158 [LO LE], Sommai Sommai/DRMS; 158 [LO RT], EBFoto/SS; 159 [UP], Skypixel/DRMS; 159 [LO LE], Chriswood44/DRMS; 159 [LO RT], Stian Olsen/DRMS; 160 [UP LE], Sahua/DRMS; 160 [UP RT], Hurst Photo/SS; 160 [LO LE], Alecrain/DRMS; 160 [LO RT], Chrispethick/DRMS; 161 [UP], United Archives/TF; 161 [LO], [BKGD], United Archives/TF; 162 [UP], Beaniebeagle/DRMS; 162 [LO LE], Michael Flippo/DRMS; 162 [LO RT], Lee6713/DRMS; 163 [UP], Ruslan Gilmanshin/DRMS; 163 [LO], Jankojerinic/DRMS; 164 [UP], Skafy1/DRMS; 164 [LO], Elena Schweitzer/SS; 165 [LO], Georgii Dolgykh/DRMS; 166 [UP LE], Chrishowey/DRMS; 166 [UP RT], Action Sports Photography/SS; 166 [LO LE], Elnur/SS; 166 [LO RT], Dave Bredeson/DRMS; 167 [UP], Anankkml/DRMS; 167 [LO], Computer Earth/SS; 168 [UP], Isselee/DRMS; 168 [LO LE], Yael Weiss/DRMS; 168 [LO RT], Sebastian Kaulitzki/DRMS; 169 [LO], Michael Rosskothen/SS; 170 [LO LE], Willeecole/DRMS; 170 [LO RT], Martina Osmy/DRMS